God's Girl Says Yes

WYNTER PITTS

HARVEST HOUSE PUBLISHERS
EUGENE, OREGON

Cover Image © Vector-RGB / Shutterstock

Cover design by Design by Julia

Interior design by Janelle Coury

HARVEST KIDS is a registered trademark of The Hawkins Children's LLC. Harvest House Publishers, Inc., is the exclusive licensee of the federally registered trademark HARVEST KIDS.

God's Girl Says Yes

Copyright © 2018 by Wynter Pitts
Published by Harvest House Publishers
Eugene, Oregon 97408
www.harvesthousepublishers.com

ISBN 978-0-7369-7039-6 (pbk.)
ISBN 978-0-7369-7040-2 (eBook)

Library of Congress Cataloging-in-Publication Data is on file at the Library of Congress, Washington, DC.

Printed in the United States of America

18 19 20 21 22 23 24 25 26 / VP-JC / 10 9 8 7 6 5 4 3 2 1

Contents

Let's Be Friends!

Hi, friend.

I am so excited I get to spend time with you.

What did you do today?

Was it fun?

Oh, I get it. You think it's pretty weird to talk to a book, right? Well, it really isn't.

I know that reading a book is not the same as hanging out with your friends, but there is definitely something special about spending time with a good book. Really, a good book can be a lot like a good friend. You see, a while ago I thought of some things I wanted to tell you, and I wrote them down. That way we can talk whenever you want. In fact, I've left plenty of space for you to write down your own thoughts too. You may even want to invite a friend to be a part of our conversations and time together.

As you read each page, I want you to take your time. This isn't the kind of book you need to rush through or complete in a hurry. But you *will* want to finish it. I'll be sharing with you so many fun and exciting things, and I want to encourage you to take your time and read every word.

First, I want to talk about what it means to be God's girl and what He had in mind when He chose you to be His daughter. The best part is that I have friends—girls like you—to introduce you to. These friends' journeys are just a few examples of the amazing things God has planned for girls who follow Him.

And in case you're wondering, God has an amazing journey planned for guys too. He loves all His children and wants to give them the best life ever, which is a life with Him forever. But God's plan for guys is going to have to be another book from another friend. This one is just for us.

So, do you know what it means to follow God? Sometimes it's easy to *say* we are following God, but it's not always easy to *do*.

Following God is like a game of follow-the-leader. Well, okay, not really—but if you've played follow-the-leader, you probably know what I mean. I think, though, you'll find following God is way better than any game you will ever play. God is not only the best Leader, but He is also your Father, your Teacher, and your Friend. He is the total package, and He takes complete care of His girls. His love for you is bigger than anything you could ever imagine, and I want to talk about that love too.

So now that I've told you what I want to talk about, I am officially inviting you to join me. Pretend this invitation came in the mail in a pretty envelope—your favorite color!—with your name written on the front. This invitation is just for you, and our time together is going to be awesome.

Okay, now that I've told you what to expect, you have a choice to make.

You can close this book and not read another word of it. Or you can accept my invitation to keep reading and explore with me. We'll dig deep into all the important and fun things I want us to talk about.

I hope this isn't a difficult choice for you. Remember, I said our time together is going to be awesome. But I'll go ahead and give you a little time to think about it. You're invited, and if you want to know the awesome things I have to share, you have to say yes.

The choice is yours.

1

Chosen

Hey, that's awesome! I'm so glad you decided to keep reading! I have to say, I think you've made an excellent choice. I am so excited about spending time with you. Picture me doing a very silly, very happy dance right now. I really hope that reading this book is something you will never forget.

To be honest, I forget things all the time. I forget where I put my glasses, what I ate for dinner, and what page I was on when reading my favorite books. But there are some things I will never forget. For example, I will never forget the day I met my best friend in pre-K. We were only four years old. She started a day later than everyone else because she had ended her summer with a vacation to Disney World. I can still remember her standing at the door, staring into the classroom with a firm grip on her mother's hand. Mrs. Preston, our teacher, walked over, took her hand, and introduced her to the rest of the class. I remember thinking, "Aww, I want to be her friend." And guess what? We are still friends today.

I also remember the first time I got in trouble at school. A special guest was making a presentation at the front of the room. I was really short for my age, so I had a hard time seeing. That's why, instead of doing what the teacher asked and sitting on my bottom with my legs crossed in front of me, I kept sitting up on my knees to try to get a better view of our guest. I really wanted to make sure I didn't miss anything. After a bunch of corrections from my teacher, she decided she had asked me to sit on my bottom one too many times. She sent me to the time-out corner, and I missed the rest of the presentation. That wasn't fun at all.

How about you? What things have happened in your life that you will never forget? Maybe it's the day you met your best friend, won a talent show, or became a big sister.

Whatever you remember, it probably changed your life forever, and that's the reason it matters a lot.

In school, my favorite year was the fifth grade. I was ten years old, and many special things happened that year. But I will never forget one day in particular.

The day started a lot like any other day. I woke up, ate two waffles (my favorite!), brushed my teeth, and got dressed for school. I don't remember exactly what I wore, but it was probably wrinkled and very comfortable. When I left the house that morning, I had no idea how much my life would change.

Like I did every weekday, I spent the entire day at school. I went to math, recess, lunch, reading, and history. I passed a few notes to my friends and talked to them in the hall in between our classes. It wasn't until the very end of the school day that I realized something different was happening. When my mother picked me up, my fifth-grade teacher, Mrs. Duncan, asked to speak to her privately.

Can you guess what my first thought was?

If you said, "Uh-oh," you're right.

When I saw my teacher motion for my mother to come with her, I was scared. I was so worried! Within seconds of their private conversation, I had convinced myself I was in big trouble, but—and this is the worst part—I had no idea what I had done.

I started to replay my entire day, and some of the craziest thoughts began to run through my mind. Had I accidentally tripped someone? Did my teacher happen to see when I passed a quick note to my best friend during math? Or did someone say I did something I didn't do? I was so afraid of getting in trouble at school, and I was even more afraid of the trouble I would get in at home now that Mrs. Duncan was telling my mother all about it.

You've probably noticed that I have a pretty wild imagination. It can be fun sometimes, but it can also create a lot of worry in me.

While Mom and Mrs. Duncan talked, I continued to think and worry. I sat quietly at my desk and watched as everyone else headed home. I was terrified of the punishment I would receive for whatever rule I had unknowingly broken.

I continued to wait while Mrs. Duncan talked to my mom. I tried to hear them, but they were not talking loud enough. I also tried to read their lips, but they were too far away for me to see. All I could do was wait. And wait. And wait.

When they finished, my mother came over to me and motioned for me to come. I slowly collected my things, anxiously waiting for her to say something to me. She smiled a little, but other than telling me it was time to go, she didn't even mumble a word. I grabbed my mother's hand, waved goodbye to Mrs. Duncan, and walked out of our classroom, down the hall, and out of the school. I was puzzled.

My heart was beating really fast as I continued to try to figure out what I could have possibly done wrong. I don't remember how long it was before my mom finally told me what she and my teacher had actually talked about, but I do remember the relief I felt when I saw the huge smile on her face. Only then did I realize I wasn't in trouble at all. The idea that maybe the sudden parent-teacher conference would mean good news had not even crossed my mind until I saw a happy expression on my mother's face. And what my mother told me was good news. Very good news.

Here's what happened.

A few weeks before this incident, we had taken a big test at school. It was a very hard test that lasted all week long. It wasn't fun, and everyone—including our teachers—was really glad when it was over. I hadn't thought much about the test since then, and I didn't really want to. I actually thought everyone had forgotten all about it.

Well, I was wrong. It turns out that Mrs. Duncan had not forgotten about the test, and that was exactly what she talked to my mother about. Mrs. Duncan wanted to tell my mother I had done well and she was proud of me.

And that wasn't the only thing.

Mrs. Duncan also told my mother that because of my scores, I had been chosen to participate in a special program at a local college. As my mother was explaining all this to me, I could not stop giggling. I was only in the fifth grade, and I was already going to college.

Okay, well, not exactly.

My mother explained that the program was designed for elementary-school students. A small number of fifth graders had been invited to spend an entire day on the college campus. She assured me it was going to be a special experience, and I believed her.

As I listened to my mother tell me about her conversation, I realized I had been worrying about nothing. I wasn't in trouble. My mom and my teacher hadn't been talking about a punishment at all. Their conversation was the complete opposite of what I had imagined. But I'd spent so much time convincing myself that I had broken a rule, so it never even occurred to me that the entire conversation might actually be good news.

The truth was, Mrs. Duncan was not waiting to punish me. Instead, she wanted to reward me for doing well on the test, so she chose me to do something special.

When I think about Mrs. Duncan, I can't help but smile. I am so grateful that she chose me to participate in that very special program.

Being chosen changed everything for me. I felt special, and I thought more about the choices I made. I didn't want to waste the great opportunity I had been given.

When Mrs. Duncan chose me, I wasn't perfect, and I'm still not. I'm so glad she chose me anyway. Once I knew someone thought I was special, I felt special, and I wanted my behavior to match.

The Bible tells us that God thinks we are special. In fact, He's the One who created us that way. He has chosen us to be His daughters. That's right—God, the Creator of the world, has chosen *you* to be *His*.

In the Bible, Jesus shares a few words about God's decision to pick you. He says,

> You did not choose me. I chose you. And I gave you this work: to go and produce fruit—fruit that will last (John 15:16).

In other words, Jesus has invited you to live a very special life with God, and every choice you make matters because you have been chosen.

When I realized Mrs. Duncan had given me an amazing opportunity, I thought differently about everything I said and everything I did. This also happens when we realize that God has given us amazing opportunities too. God wants us to live a life that lets everyone else know how good He is. And He wants our lives to look like His because we are His children.

Your life has a purpose, and God has wonderful things for you to experience and very special things He wants you to do. The best part is that all you have to do is say yes.

It's really that simple. God has everything you need, and He can't wait to give it to you. All you need to do is believe that what He says is true and say yes to trusting Him. (If you're not sure what I mean, keep reading! The beginning of chapter 2 will help!)

Have you ever told God that you want everything He has for you? In other words, have you said yes to God?

God has chosen you, and He wants to give you a special life. But in order to enjoy that life, you have to choose Him too.

Let me explain.

Being chosen by God is an amazing gift.

So think of your favorite gift. How well do you take care of it? When you're not using it, do you store it in a safe place where it won't get ruined? Even though someone else purchased it or made it for you, you are the one responsible for what happens to it, right?

Well, the same is true for your life. God wants you to know that He, your Creator, has chosen you. He has chosen to teach you, to protect you, and to love you. He has chosen to give you the option of living your life according to His design. In other words, you get to take care of the life He gave you. You are now responsible for it.

Like I said, the day Mrs. Duncan chose me for that college program was unforgettable, as were many of the days after that one. I will always remember how special I felt. And that memory will always remind me of an important truth: In order for me to receive the benefits of being chosen, I had to participate. I had to get up and get dressed. I had to show up to the event, and I had to do my best while I was there.

The same is true for you. God has chosen you, and He is waiting for you to participate. He chose you, but He can't use your life to show His love for you if you don't let Him. Saying yes to Him truly is the best choice you can ever make.

2

The Best Yes

Did you know that saying yes to God is not hard?
Saying yes to God may seem difficult because you can't see His face or touch His hands. But God is not hiding way up in the clouds with a checklist of rules He wants you to follow in order to make Him happy. No way! God is much closer than you think. In fact, He is with you everywhere and all the time.

In the Bible, John 3:16 teaches that God loves you and me so much that He sent His Son, Jesus, so we can be in a forever-relationship with God. You see, you and I don't always live the way God wants us to live. (In fact, we don't even always live the way *we* want to live! We find ourselves saying and doing things we absolutely don't want to be saying or doing!) Jesus was never like that. He never sinned. Ever. But He chose to take the punishment for our sins, and that included dying on the cross.

In the Bible, you can read many verses that show you how to say yes to God.

> To all who did receive him, to those who believed in his name, he gave the right to become children of God—children born not of natural descent, nor of human decision or a husband's will, but born of God (John 1:12-13 NIV).

Who is the "him" this verse? It's Jesus! To say yes to God and become His child, let God know that you believe everything the Bible says about Him and about you. When you tell God you believe you're a sinner and thank Him for sending Jesus as the Savior, you can trust that God hears you and that you are His daughter forever. You will have been born into His family, and you have become a child of God.

One more word about our sin. Even though we all want to make good decisions, sometimes we mess up. But here's some great news—whether you're making tons of awesome choices or you seem to be making more mistakes than you can count, God will never stop loving you. He is the best Father ever!

Sometimes we spend a lot of time trying to please God or to get closer to Him by making sure that we do the right thing, but that's not what God wants. He doesn't just want our behavior to look good. He wants our hearts to be filled up with His love, and that happens when we receive Jesus as our Savior and let His love live inside of us.

I was only five years old when I first said yes to God. I don't remember the exact day, but recently my mother sent me a special reminder in the mail. It came wrapped in lots of Bubble Wrap, and when I opened it, I saw a light brown picture frame with an old piece of peach-colored paper behind the glass.

The peach paper had three different stickers on it—a Bible, a pair of praying hands, and a bumblebee with the words "Be a Helper" on it. There were a lot of other words on the paper, but these were the first ones that caught my eye:

> Wynter Evans understands the marvelous truth that
> Jesus died on the cross, was buried in the tomb, and
> rose again from the dead on the third day to give her
> abundant and eternal life.

The paper was signed and dated March 10, 1985.

Even though I was so young, I loved God, and I loved learning about Him. I believed what the Bible says—that God loves me so much that He sent His Son, Jesus, so I can be forgiven and live with Him forever.

Ever since I got that package in the mail, I have kept the frame close by. Seeing it makes me smile. It also reminds me how much Jesus loves me and how thankful I am that He does.

Even after many, many years, I am still so glad that on March 10, 1985, I said yes to loving God. It was the best decision I've made in my entire life.

I made the decision to say yes to God when I was five, but it took me a while to understand what my decision really meant. Unfortunately, sometimes I thought that saying yes to God just meant saying no to other things. I thought it was about following a lot of rules.

But having a relationship with God is definitely not the same thing as following a list of rules, hoping He will give you good things if you do what's right—and worrying that He will punish you when you don't! God has many good things for you, and He *always* wants to give them to you. His goodness to you is not based on your ability to be good. God is good to you because He is good. But it doesn't stop there. Read what else is good:

> We are God's masterpiece. He has created us anew in Christ Jesus, so we can do the good things he planned for us long ago (Ephesians 2:10 NLT).

God has good things planned for us—for you! He is inviting you to join Him on a journey He prepared for you long before you were born.

Isn't it neat to know God has a very special plan designed specifically for you? He does! And He says His plan for you is good. He wants you to live it out, and you can be confident that saying yes to His plan for your life will lead to the best life you can live.

In case you're wondering, do you know why you can believe God has good plans for you? Because God said it. He always means what He says, and He always keeps His promises.

In addition to making special plans for you, God has made you in a very special way. He calls you His masterpiece! You are one of a kind, specially handcrafted by God.

Think about your favorite doll or your favorite dessert. When I was a little girl, I had lots of dolls along my bedroom walls—and each one was my favorite! I also had a favorite dessert. Can you guess what it was? Well, I actually love anything chocolate, but chocolate bars are the best of all.

When I think about those dolls, I can't help but think about the people who made them. Each of my dolls was specially made. Each one had her own look and her own purpose. Some I would use for teatime. Others I would use for playing "family." I had a special role for each of them, and so did the person who designed them.

My chocolate bar, though, had only one use, but it was a very special one—to fill my mouth with joy and to make my tummy happy!

Well, more than any doll and even more than a chocolate bar, you are special. God made you as one of His masterpieces, and you're uniquely designed to fulfill His specific purpose for you.

Yes, God handcrafted you, and He has a special plan for your life. He wants you to walk according to that plan, and all you have to do is say yes to God one day at a time. One *yes* at a time.

And guess what a very neat part of God's plan for you is! Read this next verse and you will find out.

> It is God who works in you to will and to act in order to fulfill his good purpose (Philippians 2:13 NIV).

I think it's amazing that God puts His special plan on your heart. When you say yes to God, He begins to move your heart to act in ways that line up with His plan for you.

God created us, so He knows that the best life we can live happens when we listen to what He tells us in our hearts to do. He waits for our yes.

I want to tell you about my friends Katherine and Isabelle. They are a lot like you—they go to school every day, they love eating snacks, and they giggle at funny noises and stories. They also really enjoy doing crafts.

Sound like you? At least a little bit?

One of their favorite crafts to do with their family is origami. "Origami" is a Japanese word that means "folding paper." People have been doing this craft for thousands of years and have created some amazing designs. Have you ever seen any origami? Have you ever done origami? If you haven't, definitely give it a try!

Well, one day Katherine and Isabelle learned that people in different places around the world were getting sick and suffering because they didn't have clean water. Katherine and Isabelle were only five and eight years old, but they decided they wanted to do something to help.

After praying and brainstorming, they came up with an idea. Can you guess what it was?

They decided to find ways to sell the origami figures they loved to make. And guess what happened next? They found a store that was willing to help them sell their origami. Then they got to work creating more and more pieces until they had quite an inventory.

And people loved their work! In fact, in a short while, Katherine and Isabelle sold enough origami pieces to pay for an entire clean-water well. They were so excited to be helping people in other countries have clean water.

These girls could have stopped after paying for that one well. But God, who had first stirred their hearts to begin the project, continued stirring their hearts to make more origami so they could pay for even more wells and help even more people.

When they realized that God had given them special skills and that they could use those skills to help others, Katherine and Isabelle began to get more serious about their business. They practiced and learned how to make even bigger and more complicated designs. In just five years, they sold enough origami pieces to raise more than $1 million. They are still doing origami, and they have even created an organization, Paper for Water, to help girls and families all over the world get the water they need.

Isn't that incredible?

When other people saw what Katherine and Isabelle were doing, those people wanted to help. So now people from many different places contribute their origami in order to help others.

I love that Katherine and Isabelle saw a need and were not afraid to try to do something about it. They are perfect examples of what God can do when we say yes to Him. They had said yes to receiving God's love for them, and then, when His heart moved them to share His love with others, they said yes again. How cool!

Katherine and Isabelle are two of God's masterpieces. He gave them the perfect talent at the perfect time to help accomplish

His perfect plan. They said yes to God's plan, they started making origami, and God blessed their work.

I realize that Katherine and Isabelle's story can seem a bit overwhelming. Something so big may seem impossible to accomplish.

If you feel that way, you're not alone in thinking God could never use you in such a big way. But here are two things to remember.

First, that simply isn't true. God can choose anyone He wants to accomplish anything!

Second, you can say yes to God no matter how old you are. And when you say yes to God, other people will be able to feel His love from the way you treat them. That's what happens when you choose to live the life He has for you!

One more thing. It's important to know that loving God, saying yes to Him, does not mean every aspect of your life will be perfect. But you can absolutely trust that God is always with you and that He will always take care of you. He wants you to grow in a relationship with Him that will never end.

Maybe your story is a little bit like mine. Has someone told you how much Jesus, God's Son, loves you? Have you made the decision to believe in His forgiveness and love? Have you decided to let Him be the One who guides your life? Don't worry if you don't have a special piece of paper with the date on it. You don't have to have that in order for your yes to be true.

And you certainly don't need a piece of paper to know that God loves you. You can trust that when you said yes to God, He heard you, and He will always remember your decision to follow Him.

I also want you to know that God will never *make* you love Him. He loves you so much that He gives you opportunities to accept His love. That may sound funny, but God will not force you to choose Him. That's a decision only you can make.

If you have never made that decision and are wondering what I'm talking about, that's okay too. It's always a good time to say yes to God for the first time.

Will you pray with me?

Dear God,

Thank You so much for loving me. I believe that Jesus is Your Son and that He died for me. Thank You for giving me a chance to love You too. I want to live *with* You forever, and I also want to live *for* You right now. I am so happy to be a part of Your family, and I want to be like Jesus. Will You help me to know how? Will You show me how to follow You as I decide what I will say, how I will treat others, and what I will do? Thank You for offering me an amazing life.

In Jesus's name, amen.

I am so excited that you have prayed that prayer with me. If this is your first time telling Jesus that you believe He is God's Son, be sure to let an adult know. And know that God is smiling because of how happy this makes Him. He can't wait to spend more time with you!

3

Saying Yes to Relationship

I used to think that God needed me to grow up before He could do something amazing with my life. After all, what could I do for God when I was only five, eight, or ten years old? All I did was go to school, play (or argue) with my friends, and eat snacks all day. I never thought God would want to use me when I was a kid. I believed He could do great things through my grandmother and my mom and my uncles and my aunts.

But I thought I was supposed to focus on kid stuff. Someday I would grow up and graduate from college, and then God would be able to accomplish something important through me. But until then, I was just a little girl. At least that's what I thought.

But I had a lot of funny ideas about what my grown-up life would be like.

I imagined that every morning, after getting dressed in my gorgeous (and clean) home, I would drive my luxurious (and clean) car or take a (not very clean) taxi into the city. I would hop out of my car, gently push my dark sunglasses to the top of my head, where they would rest like a perfect headband, stroll across the parking lot, and enter a huge mirrored-glass building—the tallest building on the block. I would have a wonderful job with one of the best companies in the world. (I had no idea what the job would be or which company I would work for, but I was sure I would be doing something amazing in an amazing place.)

I would say "good morning" and politely smile at the man or woman standing at the door. Then I would take an elevator to the top floor, where I would walk down a long hallway and make a clicking sound with every step I took on those sparkling clean floors. I would be the boss, of course, so everyone would be so happy to see me. After greeting everyone with a bright grin and happy wave, I would walk into my huge office. My lovely assistant would immediately hand me a cup of hot, sugar-filled coffee as I dropped my purse on the chair behind the biggest desk you could ever imagine. Of course, from my office, the view of the beautiful city was magnificent.

I would always be wearing the trendiest outfits. One day a fancy black dress with shiny jewelry and diamond earrings. Another day, the perfect pair of jeans with a different purse to match my shoes and my outfit of the day. I would definitely and always look fabulous.

In my mind, that was exactly how I would begin every amazing day.

When I closed my eyes tightly and imagined my adult life, it was all perfect. The funny thing is, I had no clue what I actually wanted to do. I just knew what I wanted it to look like. I wanted it to be big and great, and I wanted people to know my name and to think I was great too.

And I wanted to make a lot of money.

I actually thought that having a lot of money and being the boss would make my life amazing. After all, people in charge often appear to be having the best time. So in my mind, when I was finally in charge, that would be the perfect time for God to do amazing things in my life. That would be when I could get around to helping other people. You know...doing God stuff.

But that's not quite the way things worked out.

After I graduated from college, I did not get a job in a glass building with a doorman greeting me, the well-dressed boss. No one was excited to see me in the mornings, and no assistant was handing me a cup of hot coffee. In fact, sometimes real life was exactly the opposite of what I had imagined. You see, *I* was the one fixing the coffee...in a tiny building...with a boss who didn't even know my name.

After a few years of working at a job I didn't even like, I had to ask myself, "Why didn't I become something great?" At one point, my life looked so different from what I had imagined, I even asked God why He wasn't doing the things I wanted Him to do. After all, I thought I had done what I was supposed to do and followed all the rules He wanted me to follow. What had gone wrong?

I don't know about you, but sometimes when I have a dream that doesn't come true, it becomes really easy to feel like I failed or did something wrong. So for a long time, I felt like a failure. Everyone around me seemed to be growing up and doing amazing things. Everyone but me.

As you can imagine, I was really frustrated and even sad. What had I done wrong? Why didn't God want to do something great with my life? Was God mad at me? Had He changed His mind about loving me?

Since then I've learned something that I didn't understand at the time. Now I realize—and this is huge—life is not about what I want, but about what God wants.

> What you should want most is God's kingdom and doing what he wants you to do. Then he will give you all these other things you need (Matthew 6:33).

You see, my yes to God was missing something important, something absolutely essential: I didn't really have a relationship with Him. Even though I had said yes to God, I wasn't looking to Him for guidance or trying to learn what He wanted me to do or how He wanted me to live. I had come up with my own plans and set out to make them happen. I was also very focused on the things around me that looked appealing.

Clearly, I hadn't understood what saying yes to God really meant. Saying yes to God isn't a one-time event. It's more than saying a prayer, signing a piece of paper, and putting it in a frame. God wanted to change my life forever: He wanted to change my heart, my dreams, and my priorities. I had said yes to God, but I hadn't realized that was only the beginning, just the first in a lifelong chain of yeses.

Our initial yes to God doesn't only get you and me something (forgiveness of sin and eternal life). Our first yes to God *makes* us something. It makes you and me part of God's family.

Choosing God doesn't mean you now have to follow a list of rules in order to make Him happy. No! Choosing God means choosing to have a 24/7 relationship with Him—that means all day, every day! Choosing God means saying yes or no to His plan for you in every decision you make.

Having a relationship with God also means that you spend time with Him because you want to, because you love Him. The more time you spend with Him, the easier it becomes to say yes to whatever He asks you to do. Think of it this way...

If you have a best friend, I'm sure you don't have a list of rules to follow in order to enjoy your time together, right? That would be silly.

And no one makes you hang out with your best friend. You do it because you enjoy spending time with each other. You also enjoy doing special things together and making each other smile. For example, if your friend loves chocolate ice cream, you might surprise her with a gift of chocolate ice cream just because you love her. Not because she makes you do it, but because you like making her happy.

Well, the same principle applies in your relationship with God.

God wants to be the Friend you enjoy being around and the Friend you enjoy making smile. As you spend more time with Him, you'll get to know Him better and find out what He likes. You'll also learn that God wants more for you—more for your life—than your simply making certain choices according to certain rules. He wants you to show your love for Him by loving the people around you. After all, when we choose to say yes to Him, His love grows in our hearts.

So when does God think you are great? When you make a lot of money, wear fabulous clothes, or have a great job? There is nothing wrong with those things, but they don't affect the way God feels about you. He thinks you are great no matter what your income, your wardrobe, or your job is! Besides, God wants far more for you than a lot of money or nice clothes or a great career. He wants to have a relationship with you—He wants to be such a close friend to you that you automatically know what

He wants you to do. When we make our relationship with God the most important part of our life, then—as Jesus said in Matthew 6:33—God "will give you all these other things you need."

My dream as a little girl wasn't necessarily a bad dream. But it was *my* dream for my life, not God's dream for my life. His dream was very different from mine. And guess what? I've discovered that God's dream for me is way better than I ever could have imagined it being.

God's plan is for you and me to grow in our relationship with Him. When we first said yes to God—when we first received Him—we accepted His invitation to join Him in a loving friendship. And something really interesting happens when you spend a lot of time with someone. Do you know what it is?

If you said, "You start to act alike," you are absolutely correct. (That's one reason we need to be careful about who we're hanging out with!)

When you hang out a lot with someone, you start acting like that person. You may talk the way she does or do things the way she does. That's why people who are a part of the same family often act a lot alike. They aren't even trying—over time, it just starts to happen.

Think about it. Do some people in your family say the same phrases, laugh the same way, or move their hands the same way when they talk? Maybe you and your sister were telling a story together, and you said the exact the same thing at the exact same time. (I love when that happens!)

When I was a little girl, people often told me I looked like my mother. In fact, they still do. However, now they also tell me I act like her. The truth is, I don't even need anyone to tell me because I already know I do. Without even thinking about it, I sometimes move my hands the way she does when she talks. I put lotion on my feet every night before bed, just like she does. I even chew like she chews. I think it is so interesting...because my mother never actually taught me to do these little things. She just did them a lot, and now I do too—simply because we spent time together. I do other things, though, not only because of time we spent together but because I know her, and I know what makes her happy. I love making my mother smile.

Well, I'm sure you know where I'm going with this talk about Mom. What happens because I've spent time with my mother—I act like her, I know what makes her happy—also happens when I spend time with God. There are some things I do and some choices I make because I know they will please Him. For example, I know that God loves seeing me be grateful for the things I have, all of which He's given me! He also loves hearing me sing to Him and praise Him. (I may not sound great, but I love singing for Him!)

And sometimes I do other things simply because I am part of His family. I act like Him even when I'm not trying to. Sometimes, for instance, He helps me not get mad, or I'm able to be more patient when I'm annoyed. God loves when these moments happen because He wants the people around me to see me act like Him and know that I am in His family.

Of course—and you already know this—I don't always look and sound the way God would. Sometimes I get too focused on what I want, what I think I need, or where I want to go. Me, me, me. God always gives me another chance and reminds me that none of us can act like Him without His help. But as we spend time with God and practice saying yes to Him—as we enjoy our relationship with Him—He will give us everything we need to be more and more like Him.

Dear God.

Thank You for calling me to be Your child, for forgiving my sin and guaranteeing me eternal life with You in heaven. I ask that You would help me walk closely with You, my heavenly Father and my Friend. I want to know You better. I want to be able to recognize Your voice and Your guidance. I want to say yes when You direct my path. I want to make You a proud parent. And I want people to see the family resemblance as I become more like You. I love You.

In Jesus's name, amen.

Before we continue, I think now would be a good time to tell you what I believe about God's love for us and about who Jesus is. The verses I'll share with you help explain why I believe what I believe.

1. Jesus, God's Son, came to the earth to give us a rich life on earth and eternal life with Him in heaven.

> Life comes from the Father himself. So the Father has also allowed the Son to give life (John 5:26).

2. Jesus is completely human at the same time He is completely God.

> No one can see God, but the Son is exactly like God. He rules over everything that has been made (Colossians 1:15).

3. God loves you so much that He sent Jesus to die for you.

> God loved the world so much that he gave his only Son, so that everyone who believes in him would not be lost but have eternal life (John 3:16).

4. God's girls—His daughters, you and I—say yes to following His Spirit.

> The true children of God are those who let God's Spirit lead them (Romans 8:14).

5. God helps us.

> Jesus has the power of God. And his power has given us everything we need to live a life devoted to God. We have these things because we know him. Jesus chose us by his glory and goodness (2 Peter 1:3).

4

Saying Yes to God's Help

Have you ever read about the Israelites in your Bible? Well, the story of the Israelites is not just *a* story—it's *your* story. (And mine.) It's a story about choices. It's the story of God's choice to love a certain group of people—the Hebrew nation—and have a relationship with them. And it's about His promises to them.

You can read some of their story starting in Genesis 12. It continues until the end of Genesis and through the entire book of Exodus. I encourage you to choose a version of the Bible that's easy to read, like the New Century Version, the New Living Translation, or the New International Version. Maybe you already have one of these or a version you like. Maybe you can ask your mom or dad if you can read the Bible online. Anyway, for now, let me give you a quick summary of the story here.

The story of the Israelites begins with a man named Abraham. And God chose Abraham just like He chose you.

> Abram was ninety-nine years old when the
> LORD appeared to him again and said, "I am
> God All-Powerful. If you obey me and always
> do right, I will keep my solemn promise to
> you and give you more descendants than can
> be counted" (Genesis 17:1 CEV).

God loved Abraham and asked Abraham to obey Him and do right. He promised never to leave Abraham and even to give him as many family members as there are stars in the sky. This might sound like a weird promise to you, but having lots of children was a huge blessing in Abraham's culture. The more children you had, the more helpers your family would have, and the more success you could have in your farming, carpentry shop, tent making, or trading. Children were also a sign of God's blessing.

Abraham trusted God, and God kept His promise. God gave Abraham a huge family, starting with his son Isaac and growing Abraham's family into the nation of Israel, which still exists today.

In the book of Deuteronomy, God gave the Israelites a choice—an invitation to say yes to Him.

> Today I have given you a choice between life
> and death, success and disaster. I command
> you today to love the LORD your God. I com-
> mand you to follow him and to obey his commands,
> laws, and rules. Then you will live, and your nation
> will grow larger. And the LORD your God will bless you
> in the land that you are entering to take for your own.
> But if you turn away from your God and refuse to lis-
> ten, if you are led away to worship and serve other
> gods, you will be destroyed (Deuteronomy 30:15-18).

God gave the Israelites this choice—they could love Him, or they could love other gods. Of course, there is really only one God. But if we choose to love anything else more than we love Him, that thing is called a god (with a small "g").

God promised the Israelites that if they loved Him—and that would be evident in their obeying Him—He would lead them to a great land, to the Promised Land. It's called Israel, and you can find it on a map today. I've actually been there, and it is beautiful. God also promised to bless the Israelites and give them success in everything they did.

It would take a really long time to read the Israelites' entire story. Trust me when I say it has a lot of ups and downs, successes and failures, wins and losses. When the Israelites made good decisions, God blessed them—as He had promised. When they made bad decisions, God let them suffer the consequences of their disobedience.

But God's promises never fail, so all the way through the Israelites' story, God never left them. In fact, He always looked for ways to help them. That story went on for thousands of years, and it is still going on today.

The Israelites' story shows us how difficult it is to make good choices all the time. Sometimes saying yes day after day after day after day can be really hard. I bet you can relate. Every day you face a lot of choices. In fact, research says you face about 3,000 decisions a day. That's how many times you say yes or no.

You make choices even when you aren't thinking about it.

You choose to obey or disobey your parents.

You choose to do your homework or waste time.

You choose to walk or run.

You choose to gossip or walk away.

You choose to react in anger or in love.

The whole point of God's story and His friendship with Israel is that He loves His people and wants His people to choose Him. He entered into a relationship with Israel on purpose. He knew what was best for them, and He knows what is best for you.

But God also knows that making good choices is sometimes difficult. So God gave the Israelites another promise—something even better than lots of kids and a beautiful land to live in. God promised Israel a Savior who would save them from the power of sin and death. God promised them Jesus.

God knew that the Israelites would not be able to say yes all the time. He knew that they would often choose to worship other gods rather than stay close to Him. He also knew that their poor choices would get them into trouble, and that made Him sad. The only way God could help them make better choices was to change their hearts. So to do that...

> God has sent his special servant Jesus. He sent him to you first. He sent him to bless you by causing each of you to turn away from your evil ways (Acts 3:26).

In this verse, the word "you" refers to Israel.

In short, God sent Jesus to Israel so the people could be changed from the inside out. A changed heart would mean changed thoughts, words, and actions. This inner change was God's plan to help keep His people from making bad decisions, to keep them from sinning. And through the family line of the

Israelites, God sent Jesus to us. Jesus saves us from our bad choices—from our sins.

God chose to help Israel back then, and He chooses to help you (and me) today.

We have seen that we begin our relationship with Jesus by saying yes to Him. Well, here's what's really cool—when we first say yes to following Jesus, He helps us continue saying yes in the future!

God wants to have a relationship with you, and that's why He sent Jesus to help you avoid mistakes, to choose obedience, and to never be separated from God because of your sins. You can completely trust Jesus to help you obey God and make your relationship with Him your most important priority. And you can trust Jesus because Jesus wasn't just a man. Jesus came to earth as a man, but He was also called Immanuel, which means "God with us." Jesus was and is God. He came from heaven to help you and me.

But now that Jesus has returned to heaven, how can He continue to change us from the inside out? How can He work in us to make us more like Him so we can continue saying yes to Him?

After Jesus died for us, rose from the dead, and returned to His Father, Jesus sent us a Helper we call the Holy Spirit. With the gift of His Spirit, Jesus made a way for us to continue having a relationship with Him even after He left the earth to be with Father God. Here is what Jesus said to His disciples shortly before He died:

> I will ask the Father, and he will give you another Helper, to be with you forever...The Helper will teach you everything and cause you to remember all that I told you. This Helper is the Holy Spirit that the Father will send in my name (John 14:16,26).

I'm going to tell you a funny sounding truth: God wants to grow inside of you. He wants to be so big inside of you that you pop open and spill His love everywhere you go. God starts growing inside you when you say yes to Him. He lives in you through His Spirit—the Holy Spirit.

God has chosen you to have His love inside of you. He's also chosen you to share His love with everyone around you.

Loving people doesn't happen automatically when you try to follow all God's rules and laws. The Israelites couldn't do that, and neither can we. God had to help Israel over and over and over again, and He did this by sending leaders and prophets to His people and by performing mighty miracles to encourage their faith in Him. God also chooses to help you over and over and over again, but He has chosen to help you by living inside you through His Spirit.

Saying yes to Jesus is actually a lifelong process that looks something like this:

God the Father chose you.

The Father sent Jesus to you as a gift.

You receive Jesus as a gift.

Jesus sent the Holy Spirit as another gift and a helper.

The Holy Spirit lives inside you to help you do what God wants you to do.

Through the Holy Spirit in you, God shares Himself with others.

The Spirit gives you access to Jesus, and Jesus gives you access to the Father.

Now you can hang out with God—the Father, the Son (Jesus), and the Holy Spirit. The more time you spend with God, the bigger He grows in you.

The good news really is this simple.

Dear God,

Thank You for the example of Abraham. You made him an amazing promise that looked impossible for a long time, but Abraham trusted You. And You kept Your promise. I want to trust You the way Abraham did, so I thank You for giving us Your Holy Spirit. Thank You that He is at work changing my heart. Thank You for this Helper, who will help me avoid mistakes, choose obedience, and keep saying yes to You. Please help me remember to rely on my Helper.

In Jesus's name, amen.

5

Saying Yes to Being Fruitful

What is God like?

The Bible tells us that Jesus came to show us God's love. When we see Jesus loving people, forgiving them, and accepting them into His family, we can know that Jesus is showing us what our heavenly Father is like.

The Bible also describes God's personality by listing some of His character traits. These same character traits can grow in us—just like fruit grows on a tree—because God's Spirit lives in us. That's why these characteristics are called the fruit of the Spirit. Yes, God actually wants to grow inside of you. How cool is that! He makes some of His traits come alive in you when you say yes to Jesus and when you continue saying yes to Him every day.

When you say yes, God gives you the power to experience His life—His Spirit—in you!

The Bible says that we can know if someone is God's child by the way she lives and by the fruit growing in her life. When you become a part of God's family, you start to become more and more like Him because His love grows in your heart. God's love changes you from the inside out. His Spirit changes the way you think, the way you act, and even the way you feel. God wants His presence inside us growing so that others will see Him—will see the fruit of His presence in us—when they look at us.

Now, before you start thinking we're talking about apples and strawberries, let me explain.

Do you know what some of the fruit of the Spirit are? Take a few minutes to name as many as you can. The Bible lists nine.

1. Love
2. gentleness
3. faithfulness
4. joy
5. Kindness
6. Self control
7. peace
8. patience
9. goodness

Don't worry if you can't name all or even any of them. We can find them in the Bible:

> The fruit that the Spirit produces in a person's life is love, joy, peace, patience, kindness, goodness, faithfulness, gentleness, and self-control (Galatians 5:22-23).

Now, the fruit of the Spirit are not just nice words that describe God—they are actually who God is. In other words, God *is* love. God *is* joy. God *is* peace. God *is* patience. God *is* kindness. God *is* goodness. God *is* faithfulness. God *is* gentleness, and God *is* self-control.

And because this is who God the Father is, it is also who Jesus is. You can say Jesus is love. Jesus is joy. Jesus is peace. Jesus is patience. Jesus is kindness. Jesus is goodness. Jesus is faithfulness. Jesus is gentleness. And Jesus is self-control.

And because this is who God the Father is and who Jesus is, this is who the Holy Spirit is and who the Holy Spirit helps you to become. Get it?

Let me put it this way. If you are saying yes to God, then this fruit is growing in you. He wants to grow all of His characteristics in you. He wants you to be full of His love, joy, peace, patience, kindness, goodness, faithfulness, gentleness, and self-control.

Have you ever tasted a rotten piece of fruit? Maybe a squishy brown grape or a black banana? They don't taste very good, do they?

Well, unlike regular fruit, Jesus's fruit never goes bad, and it will never taste bad. The fruit Jesus produces is always good.

In other words, saying yes to God and being connected to Him keeps your life from tasting like a rotten grape!

Think about your life as a big piece of fruit. Are your words, actions, thoughts, and attitudes like juicy red apples, sitting in the middle of a kitchen table, that hungry people see and want? Seeing and experiencing the fruit of the Spirit through you will give people around you a taste of Jesus. They can get a glimpse of how good God is just by being around you.

The fruit God grows inside you is different from any personality trait you can try to develop on your own. Your best efforts to be kind, patient, gentle, or good won't get you even close to what God's Spirit will do if you stay connected to Him and say yes to whatever He is doing in your life.

As I mentioned earlier, I am definitely not perfect. So I don't always make great choices. Sometimes I make not-so-great choices. However, I am grateful to know that God loves me no matter what. He doesn't expect me to be perfect. He wants me to ask Him for help when I need it.

And when you and I stay close to God, He can completely change our character. Your character is your personality—the way you think and feel, the way you speak and act and treat others. Our character is very important no matter how old we are!

Let's think about that for a minute.

What type of person do you want to be? If someone were to describe you, what four words would you want them to say?

1. _Good Christian_
   Caring
2. _Kind_
   loving
3. _funny_

4. _____

Did you write words like "sweet," "loving, "nice," "funny," and "thoughtful"? If you did, then we have a lot in common because I want people to use words like that to describe me too.

But have you ever noticed how easy it is to *want* to be something, but how hard it can be to actually *live* that way? Have you ever set an alarm at night, fully intending to get up when it started to beep and then go for a run, pray for a few minutes, or look over your notes for your science test? You and I both know that when morning comes and we're snuggled under our cozy blankets, choosing to get up when the beeping begins is very hard to do. Right?

That's exactly how it can be with becoming the type of person we want to be. I really want to be a nice person, don't you? I want to be kind, joyful, and patient with the people around me, and I want to show love to everyone. But choosing to be those things is not always easy, and sometimes I need a little help. Actually, sometimes I need a lot of help.

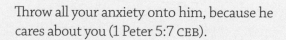

With more than 3,000 decisions to make every single day, and no one telling you how to make most of them, how can you know what's right or wrong? How can you know what will be good for you now and later? We have so many decisions to make, and that can make us feel very alone.

But wait! We have *great* help—we actually have the *greatest* Helper.

Remember, God sent the Holy Spirit for the very purpose of helping you. God cares about all of your decisions—the big ones *and* the small ones—and He is ready, willing, and able to help you with every single one of them.

Do you believe me? Take a look at this verse:

> Throw all your anxiety onto him, because he cares about you (1 Peter 5:7 CEB).

I love this verse and the picture it paints. You see, to throw something means to get rid of it. God is telling you in this verse that He is ready to catch all your anxieties and worries as you throw them His way. In fact, speaking through His disciple Peter, God is *inviting* you to throw all your cares on Him. He doesn't want just a handful or only a few. He is inviting you to throw *all* of your concerns to Him.

You can throw your cares, worries, and choices to God because He cares deeply about you and loves to help you in every and any situation.

Take a few minutes and answer this question. (You can be honest. No one is peeking). When I have a choice to make...

1. I always check the rules first.

2. I do whatever feels like the right thing to do.

3. I ask someone around me for help.

4. I pray.

It's okay if you didn't choose only one of the above options. Many choices—especially big ones—require you to do a combination of some of these things

Remember, no one has all the answers, no matter how smart, kind, or nice they are. I definitely don't always know what to do, and I have made some pretty bad choices before.

But here's the good news. We don't have to have all the answers, and we don't have to make the best choice every time. That pressure would be exhausting.

Here's more good news. When it comes to your character, your obedience, and the 3,000 decisions you make each day, you really only have to do one thing. You really only have one choice to make.

Do you want to know what it is?

Your best choice is always to say yes to God and to follow Him.

You can simply ask yourself what Jesus would do in this situation, and then ask the Holy Spirit to help you decide. The Spirit might remind you of a Bible verse you recently read, or He might tell you to ask your parents. He might even give you the right thought at the right time.

In every decision, God knows what is best for you. He wants to lead you along the path He has for your life, not the path you think is best in the moment. We follow God by taking one step at a time, and the first step is to bring Him into our decision making.

As you say yes to the things God asks you to say yes to, you will have to say no to other things—to things that are unhelpful and that He doesn't want for you. When you say yes to God and walk with Him on the path He has chosen for you, amazing things can happen.

So what do you need to remember about saying yes to God and letting His fruit grow in your life?

- Say yes to Jesus. When you initially say yes to Jesus, He will begin to grow His fruit in you. As you say yes along the way, He will continue to grow His fruit in your heart and in your life.

- Remember, it is God's fruit, not yours. Doing your best is good, but your best has human limitations, so it can fail you. God will never fail you. Depend on Him all the time, and ask Him to keep producing more fruit in your life.

- When you face big decisions, throw all your cares on Almighty God. Sometimes you will know right away what to do because God has already shown you.

Other decisions will be a little more difficult, so talk to Him in prayer and read your Bible.

- Listen for the Holy Spirit to speak to you. He can talk to you in many ways, such as giving you an idea or using the words of a parent, a friend, or a teacher. And the Spirit will never give you an answer that doesn't help you live with more love, joy, and peace. His guidance will always result in more spiritual fruit.

Maybe this idea of letting the fruit of the Spirit grow in you is new to you. That's okay because in the pages ahead, we'll learn about how each characteristic can develop in our lives. I pray that as you keep reading, God will help you to learn more about Him and the character He wants to develop in you.

Dear God,

Thank You for producing the fruit of Your Spirit inside me. I know I don't always act or speak the way You would act or speak. Sometimes I may even be more like a rotten grape, but I am so glad that You love me and want to help me be more like You. Please fill me with Your love, joy, peace, patience, kindness, goodness, faithfulness, gentleness, and self-control. I want my actions and words to give people a taste of You.

In Jesus's name, amen.

Do you read your Bible very much? Maybe a little? Sometimes a lot? Well, did you know that the Bible is the most important book you will ever read?

It's written just for you, it has the right answer to every question you will ever ask, and it will help you make the best choice in every situation you will ever face.

It's simply an awesome book.

The Bible is also full of amazing stories about God and His people. Reading your Bible is a great way to spend time with God. You can learn so much about Him by reading accounts of other people's lives. Everything in the Bible was written by God to help you understand Him and His love for His children.

In addition to the stories in the Bible, God is writing stories in our lives too. I love that God wants my life and yours to be stories of His love.

Sometimes it can be easy to forget that the people in the Bible were a lot like you and me. They were humans. Sometimes they made good choices, and sometimes they made mistakes. However, God continued to use them, and He wants to use us too.

Some of my favorite stories in the Bible are about Jesus, God's Son, coming to earth to live with people. Even though Jesus was God's Son, He was also a man. Of course He was not like any other man or woman you will ever meet, but in some ways, He was like you and me.

For example, the Bible tells us that Jesus had some great friends—and also that He had plenty of enemies who wanted to hurt Him. We read in the Bible that Jesus ate when He was hungry, He cried when He was sad, and He spent time with God when He had decisions to make. Only after praying and listening for God's direction did Jesus know what He needed to do.

Jesus never did anything without talking to God first, and then He did only the things that God, His Father, wanted Him to do.

> Jesus answered, "I assure you that the Son can do nothing alone. He does only what he sees his Father doing. The Son does the same things that the Father does" (John 5:19).

Jesus knew what God wanted Him to do because He spent time with God. When Jesus needed help making the right choice, He prayed and asked God to help Him. Relying on God's guidance, Jesus spent His life helping the people around Him and teaching them all about God's love.

Finally, Jesus did some pretty awesome things while He lived on earth. (Have you ever told the wind and waves to stop? Have you ever made a blind man see or a lame man walk?) And Jesus wants to do even more incredible things today through His people, through you and me. You don't even need to wait until you are grown up! God can do some great things with your life—and my life—right now!

All we have to do is continue saying yes to God.

6

Saying Yes to Love

In the Bible, the apostle Paul wrote a letter to his friends living in Galatia. One of the things he wrote to them about was the importance of letting God's Spirit live inside them. That's when Paul listed the fruit of the Spirit, and Paul began with love. I'm so glad that's where he started because I love knowing that God loves me!

I'm sure you've told someone—Mom, Dad, Grandma, Grandpa, your BFF—you love them. You probably say, "Love you!" almost every day. And you know all of us love to hear that we're loved! From time to time you probably also say, "I love that!"—and "that" can be a restaurant, a movie, a dog breed, a band, or even a teacher. "Love" is a popular word, and we use it all the time when we're talking about all kinds of things. Do we really love sleeping in on Saturday morning the same way we love Mom? Do we love the smell of the ocean the way we love God?

Often when we think of love, we think of pink hearts, red roses, kind words, and big hugs. We also think of people who make us smile, places we like to visit, or our favorite foods to eat. All those things are awesome, but saying that we love them doesn't give us a clear or accurate picture of what love is.

You see—and as you've probably noticed—it's not always easy to love people. And if we're saying yes to God, we need to learn how to love people even when we don't want to or we don't feel like it.

So we need to understand that love is more than a feeling. In fact, the Bible describes love as a person.

Can you guess who that person is?

The Bible tells us that love not only comes from God but that God is love.

> Dear friends, let us continue to love one another, for love comes from God. Anyone who loves is a child of God and knows God. But anyone who does not love does not know God, for God is love (1 John 4:7-8 NLT).

God is always love; He can't possibly act in any other way. Everything about God is love and loving. So whenever you think about the word "love," think about God. And because we are His children and are choosing to live in relationship with Him, He wants us to love Him so much that we cannot help but show His love to the people around us.

God knew, however, that we would understand His love better if He revealed it to us in a special way, so He did exactly that. God taught us about His love—His unconditional, compassionate, sacrificial love—by giving us the living example of His Son, Jesus. God also helps us understand His love by describing it in the Bible. Here are a few things the Bible teaches us about God's love.

1. God's love is altogether different from any other kind of love we know.

> God proves His own love for us in that while we were still sinners, Christ died for us! (Romans 5:8 HCSB).

God's love is gracious—it is the kind of love no one deserves. Not me and not you. Not nice people or successful people or beautiful people or people who work at a church. We don't have to earn God's love and, no one has to earn ours.

2. God will never stop loving you.

> Who shall separate us from the love of Christ? Shall trouble or hardship or persecution or famine or nakedness or danger or sword? (Romans 8:35 NIV).

God loved you before you were born, and nothing you will ever do can change His love for you. God loves you no matter what, and He promises to love you forever. So even when we choose not to love God, He still loves us.

Doesn't it feel great to know that God loves you no matter what? God loves everyone, all the time, even when they don't love Him back.

3. God sent Jesus because of His love.

> This is how God loved the world: He gave his one and only Son, so that everyone who believes in him will not perish but have eternal life (John 3:16 NLT).

God's love for His children is so big that He sent His Son, Jesus, to save us from the consequences of our sin, which is separation from God. God sent Jesus to be the perfect sacrificial Lamb who would die so our sins would be forgiven. God wants us to be in relationship with Him now and forever. He never wants us to be away from Him.

People who know God's love, for instance, can look a little weird when they show love and kindness to people who are mean or who mistreat them. But when God is producing His love in your life and you begin to understand God's love, you can rely on His power to love even those people who are hard to love.

And speaking of hard to love, sometimes when you say yes to loving someone else, you have to say no to yourself. Let me explain.

I only have one sibling. His name is Sean, and he's five years older than me. I've always loved having a big brother. We spent a lot of time together growing up, and he taught me how to do some pretty amazing things. However, sometimes it wasn't that fun growing up together. If you have any brothers or sisters, you won't be at all surprised to learn that Sean and I didn't always get along. Whenever Sean did something or said something that hurt my feelings, I got very upset. And although I don't like to admit it, I often wanted to find a way to hurt him back, and sometimes I would. I'd say something really mean or do something that I knew irritated him. One day, when Sean did something very mean to me, I yelled some very unkind words to him. After I said them, I felt terrible.

Even before I said the words and even as I was saying them, I knew I shouldn't have. Yes, Sean was mean to me first, but that didn't make it okay for me to be mean to him. Bottom line, God wants us to say no to what we want to do (like being mean when we've been hurt) and to say yes to what He tells us to do ("Love one another"). This may actually be one of the hardest ways to show people God's love.

If you want to know how to love the people around you even when they are not kind and loving to you, read about how Jesus treated people. In the Bible books called Matthew, Mark, Luke, and John, you'll see that Jesus is the perfect example of love. He loved everyone, all the time.

Here are a few ways Jesus loved the people around Him.

He served those in need.

> Do as I did: The Son of Man did not come for people to serve him. He came to serve others and to give his life to save many people (Matthew 20:28).

He said only what God told Him to say.

> What I taught was not from myself. The Father who sent me told me what to say and what to teach (John 12:49).

He showed God's love to everyone.

> Come to me, all you who are weary and burdened, and I will give you rest (Matthew 11:28 NIV).

God wants to grow His love in your heart, and He wants you to show His love with your actions. God wants you to show the same kind of love He does, and that's the kind you can't share without His help. The only way you can show this kind of love is to know God and have His Spirit inside you.

God asks us to show His love to others every minute of every day. That means that at several points throughout the day, we can choose to love or not to love. We can say yes, or we can say no. Saying yes to showing love is not always easy, but I want you to think about Jesus. Remember how much He loves us? And He loves us no matter what, right? Well, God wants to help us love like that too. And with His help, we can!

Here are a few questions you can think about to get started...

- What would it look like if you said yes to loving the hard-to-love person in your life today?
- What will you do today to serve someone?
- What will you do to rely on God's help to say only the things He wants you to say?
- Who will you show God's love to?

Remember, God wants us to show love all the time—not only when we feel like it and not only when someone is kind and loves us first. Instead, because we are His daughters, God wants His love that is growing inside of us to come out of us every minute we're awake.

We can't love this way—we can't love the way God does—without His help. But the good news is that God is with us—His Spirit is living inside us—and He is *always* ready to help us say yes to love!

Dear God,

Thank You for loving me. You love me when I make good choices, and You love me when I don't. I am so grateful to know that I can never do anything to make You stop loving me. And I ask You to teach me how to love like You do. I want to love others, and I want them to know how much You love them too. I know I can't do that without You. But with Your Spirit living inside me and with Your love filling me to overflowing, I can!

In Jesus's name, amen.

7

Saying Yes to Joy

I hope you know the fun song that starts like this: "I've got the joy, joy, joy, joy down in my heart. Where? Down in heart..." (Trust me! It's a good thing you can't hear me singing right now!) The upbeat tune and the hand motions do make this a fun song for everyone. But more important, the words are full of truth.

Joy, like love, is much more than something you feel when everything is going great. Joy is something you can have however hard life is at the moment when you remember that you are God's chosen daughter. And, like love, joy grows in your heart because God lives in you.

Joy is a fruit of the Spirit.

When I was little girl, I sang that joy-joy-joy song all the time. My family and I sang it in church, at home, and in the car. But it took me a long time to realize that even when things around me were sad and life was hard, I could still have the joy I was singing about.

A lot of sad things happened where I grew up. My neighborhood wasn't very safe, and we didn't have a lot of money. My mother, my brother, and I lived with my grandmother. I was grateful for a warm home to live in, but it wasn't fancy. Even with these not-so-good circumstances, my grandmother always seemed to have the biggest smile on her face. Even when everyone knew things weren't good, she remained joyful.

I didn't understand how she could do that. I don't know about you, but sometimes I feel miserable just because I have to do things I don't want to do, like take a test or fold my laundry. So how did my grandmother manage to keep smiling in her difficult situation?

You know the answer. She relied on God to give her the strength she needed, and He gave her His joy. My grandmother was full of joy because of her relationship with God. The joy that God gives does not depend on anyone else's actions or your circumstances. Joy comes from God living in us, and the joy is there regardless of what is happening around us. And the Bible tells us that God's joy makes us strong.

> Do not grieve, for the joy of the LORD is your strength (Nehemiah 8:10 NIV).

I can remember seeing my grandmother sitting quietly on the edge of her bed with tears streaming down her face. That may not sound happy to you, and it didn't seem that way to me either. But whenever I asked her what was wrong, she would smile (even with tears) and say, "Oh, I'm talking to Jesus."

I was so confused by her answer. I never really understood

what she meant or why talking to Jesus would make her cry. I thought talking to Jesus was supposed to fix the bad things that were happening around us.

Well, now I understand exactly what she was saying. My grandmother knew that she was God's child, and because of that, she had joy inside. She simply had to say yes to the joy God had made available to her. Even though things were hardly picture perfect, Mama's joy was not connected to good things or bad things. Her joy was connected to God Himself. The circumstances of our lives will change all the time, but we can have joy in our hearts because God never changes. We have joy because of who lives inside us; our joy doesn't depend on what is happening around us.

Not many people understood how my grandmother could smile so much, and she was always eager to explain it to them. She loved telling people about Jesus and the joy she had because of His love. Having joy in her heart helped her be grateful in any situation—and it can help us too. Also, my grandmother was always willing to help people around her even when she needed help herself. And Mama gave me a real-life example of this verse:

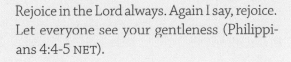

Rejoice in the Lord always. Again I say, rejoice. Let everyone see your gentleness (Philippians 4:4-5 NET).

Do you see the connection between joy and gentleness? How would you treat those around you if you always remembered that God's joy is in your heart?

I'm thinking you would not have to be mean when someone says something unkind to you or about you. You wouldn't have to feel sad because of anything people do. And you wouldn't have to worry when bad things happen. And bad things do happen. When they happen to you, remember that joy is still available. You can choose joy.

And God wants to help you make that choice. When you are feeling sad because of something, talk to God about it instead of worrying. And while you're talking, ask Him to help you know His joy.

One more thing. You can also choose joy when you're going about your everyday life. Maybe your parents have asked you to do some chores, and you really don't want to. Even then, you can choose joy. You can thank God for your family and your home and your opportunity to be helpful.

What are a few other ways you can choose joy today? After all...

- God loves you.
- God sent Jesus to bring—among other things—joy to this world.
- Jesus left His Spirit of joy with us when He returned to the Father.
- We can continue to have joy because Jesus is alive!

Dear God,

I know about feeling happy when things are going great, and I know about feeling sad when things aren't going well. Thank You for making it possible for me to have joy in *any* situation because You love me, You forgive me, and You promise to take care of me. Help me not to worry, but always to trust You. Thank You for using Your joy to make me strong. Thank You for helping me say yes to joy today!

In Jesus's name, amen.

Andy and Andrea Said Yes

Andy and Andrea are twin sisters who took a trip to Peru with their family when they were ten years old. Peru is one of the largest countries in South America, and many people there are very poor. In fact, their homes are often made from dirt and rocks.

Andy and Andrea had been helping Evelyn, a little girl who lives in Peru, by sending her things she needs. The sisters knew this was a great way to show Evelyn God's love. However, they had never met Evelyn face-to-face, and this trip to Peru would give them the opportunity to finally meet her. At first, Andy and Andrea were nervous about going and a little bit afraid of visiting a new country. They didn't know what to expect, and that was pretty scary. However, after praying about it with their mom and dad, the four of them decided to say yes and travel to Peru. And Andy and Andrea are so glad they did.

While they were in Peru, Andy and Andrea met Evelyn and her entire family. They visited her home and learned that even though she speaks a different language and looks different from them, Evelyn is one of God's daughters too. When they played together, the girls realized that the three of them enjoy a lot of the same things. Evelyn even taught the sisters a few new games.

By visiting Peru, Andy and Andrea learned a lot about a new place. They also learned from Evelyn's family how to have joy even when you don't have anything else. Evelyn and her family trust God, and that's all they need. Andy and Andrea are still able to help Evelyn with food and money for school, but those things were not what gave Evelyn joy. She was full of God's joy even though she didn't have much else.

Andy and Andrea will never forget their time in Peru. They are happy to be able to help other children around the world, and they are grateful that God showed them through Evelyn and her family how to be full of His joy. Seeing Evelyn's joy made them want to have the same joy in their hearts. Andrea and Andy knew that Evelyn's joy can only come from God. When they returned home, they began to ask God to grow more of His joy in their hearts too.

God grows our joy, for instance, when we respond to His command to serve like Jesus served. So don't be afraid to look for opportunities to serve others. Then, when you do, be ready to see what God wants to teach you about Himself.

8

Saying Yes to Peace

E veryone who knows me knows I love babies. And I especially love a brand-new baby!

When they are a few days or weeks old, and their skin is still wrinkly and super soft—that's my favorite! It's so amazing to me how small these newborns are and how much they will grow in such a short amount of time. I love seeing their tiny hands and chubby toes. They smell amazing and make the cutest sounds. I could sit and stare at a newborn baby for hours...Well, at least until they start crying.

That's the thing about babies. At some point, they all cry— some of them quite loudly, while others let out little whimpers. All tiny babies have are those cries and whimpers; they can never actually tell us what's wrong. They have to wait for someone else to figure it out and eventually fix the problem. Being independent is impossible for them—they need someone to take care of their every need. Babies don't even know how to feed themselves.

Depending on someone else to provide everything you need can be really scary. Yet babies don't spend any of their time worrying about all the things they need help with or the things that might happen in the future. Babies may cry for a little while, but when a problem is fixed, they are back to being their peaceful selves.

Babies also don't worry about what's going to happen next. They learn to trust that when they have a need, someone will be there to help them. God made babies this way, and this is the way He wants us to live too.

That's right—God wants us to act like babies! Oh wait, let me explain...

God doesn't want us crying whenever we need or want something. Instead, He wants us to trust that He will take care of every single thing we will ever need. He wants us to trust Him and to experience the peace He wants to give us.

Peace is another fruit of the Spirit.

The Bible says God is the Prince of Peace. That should be no surprise because peace is part of who God is, and it's another fruit of the Spirit that He grows in our hearts.

To understand what peace is, let's start with its opposite. And the character trait that's the opposite of peace is worry. What kinds of things do you worry about? Maybe you worry about performing in front of an audience or flying in an airplane or having a really hard conversation with a friend.

We could find a lot of things to worry about; we could actually make worrying a full-time job. But the Bible explains that we don't have to worry.

> Do not be anxious about anything. Instead, in every situation, through prayer and petition with thanksgiving, tell your requests to God. And the peace of God that surpasses all understanding will guard your hearts and minds in Christ Jesus (Philippians 4:6-7 NET).

The wonderful promise in this passage is that when we choose to take all our needs, our worries, and our tears to God in prayer, He will give us His peace.

This verse does *not* mean or even suggest that we can expect God to give us everything we want. But it does assure us that we can have a grateful heart because we know that God is taking care of us.

Have you ever wanted something really bad, but you couldn't have it? If so, you know how Hannah, a woman in the Bible, felt.

You can read Hannah's entire story in the book called 1 Samuel. There, we learn that she was married to a man named Elkanah. The couple did not have any babies, but Hannah wanted a child more than anything. And to make it even worse, most of the women around Hannah had babies. One woman named Peninnah always teased Hannah and made fun of her for not having any children.

As you can imagine, this desire to have a baby but not having one sometimes made Hannah very sad. She did her best not to worry about her situation, but she never stopped wanting a baby.

Of course, you have never been teased about not having a

baby, but maybe you have been teased about being different from people around you. If you have, then you know it can be hard not to say mean things or have mean thoughts about the people teasing you. You also probably know what it feels like to worry and feel that you to have fix the problem yourself. But this was a problem Hannah could not fix.

Every year, Hannah and her family traveled to the tabernacle to worship God. During one of their visits, Hannah watched everyone with their children, and she became very sad. The Bible says that she cried because she wanted a baby so much. But instead of just worrying about her situation, Hannah turned to God. She talked to God about her problem.

Then Hannah chose to live with peace on the inside instead of worrying about what may or may not happen in her life.

> She was deeply distressed and prayed to the LORD and wept bitterly (1 Samuel 1:10 ESV).

Like a brand-new baby, Hannah cried because she had a need. Also like a newborn, Hannah depended on someone to help her: Hannah depended on God.

And you know what?

God helped her.

A priest named Eli saw Hannah praying. When she told him what was wrong, he prayed for her as well. And then...

> Eli answered, "Go in peace, and the God of Israel grant your petition that you have made to him" (1 Samuel 1:17 ESV).

Eli told Hannah to go in peace, reminding Hannah that she didn't need to worry or try to fix her problems herself. He encouraged her to remember and trust that God was in control.

God wants you to trust Him with everything too. It doesn't matter how big or small your problem is. When you feel yourself starting to worry about something, pray and ask God to help you experience His peace.

When you say yes to peace, you are choosing to rest and to wait for God to give you everything you need.

Is there something that you need to trust God with? If so, let's pray right now.

Dear God,

Thank You for being the Prince of Peace. I am so grateful that I am Your daughter and that Your peace lives inside of me. Sometimes I forget that I don't need to worry about things, or I try to fix my problems on my own. Please help me to trust You more. I thank You in advance for helping me to say no to worry and say yes to peace.

In Jesus's name, amen.

Are you having a hard time trusting God to take care of you? Here are some verses to help you trust God and say yes to peace. The more you trust God, the more you will experience His peace in your life.

> Look for the LORD and His strength;
> seek His face always (1 Chronicles
> 16:11 NIV).

> The LORD is my strength and my song,
> and he has become my salvation;
> this is my God, and I will praise Him,
> my father's God, and I will exalt Him
> (Exodus 15:2 ESV).

> Do not fear, for I am with you;
> do not be afraid, for I am your God.
> I will strengthen you; I will help you;
> I will hold on to you with My righteous
> right hand (Isaiah 41:10 HCSB).

> Trust in the LORD with all your heart,
> and do not rely on your own understanding;
> think about Him in all your ways,
> and He will guide you on the right paths
> (Proverbs 3:5-6 HCSB).

9

Saying Yes to Patience

Have you ever heard someone say, "Good things come to those who wait"? I'm not sure that is always true, but sometimes we do need to slow down, take our time, and wait for the right time to act.

For example, have you ever noticed that you make more mistakes when you rush to finish your homework? Or you miss the best part of a story if you hurry to the end? Or that you have to sweep the kitchen floor again if you don't do a good job the first time? If you are nodding your head yes to at least one of these, then you will want to keep reading. I've got a story for you!

Not long ago, my phone rang. Even though I was busy, I answered it when I saw it was my cousin, and I'm glad I did. She called to tell me she was going to be in a movie, and she wanted to know if my daughter, Alena, wanted to audition for a part in the movie too. Alena was not an actress, so this seemed like a crazy idea! But Alena decided to audition anyway—and that was only one step in a very, very, very long process. Alena had to wait six whole weeks before she found out she was chosen to play the role of Danielle Jordan in the movie *War Room*.

As you can imagine, that was a long six weeks of waiting for an answer. We had no idea what the outcome would be, so we all had to be patient.

Waiting was hard. Alena really wanted an answer, and she got tired of waiting for it. The more time passed, the easier it was to think the casting director had chosen someone else. It also became easier to stress about it and feel sad. Being sad about something is normal—that happens to all of us. However, just as Hannah prayed to God when she needed peace, we can seek God when we need patience.

Alena knew that God wanted her to talk to Him about the movie. So instead of feeling sad, Alena prayed that God would help her trust Him and His timing. Alena prayed for patience, and so did I.

Learning how to be patient is one part of trusting God and saying yes to His plan for your life.

If you struggle with being patient, you are not alone. I, for instance, am actually not a fan of long things—long lines, long days, long books, long walks...Get the idea?

I like things to happen as quickly as possible. So I would say that being patient is definitely a fruit of the Spirit that I have to ask for help with all the time—and I am so glad God is always willing to help me, no matter how many times I ask. He has also taught me that some things take time, and it's best to wait to for them.

When I'm having a hard time being patient, I love reading about Abraham, one of God's chosen sons. (You can read about Abraham's life in Genesis 12–25.) God promised Abraham and his wife Sarah that they would have a child. But they were very old, and it didn't look like God's plan was going to happen.

In fact, the Bible says that when God told Abraham and Sarah they would get pregnant with a son, they both laughed. They had already waited years for God to do what He had promised to do, and now it seemed impossible. (I mean, Sarah was 90 years old!) God wanted Sarah and Abraham to trust Him; they needed to be patient.

> "Abraham, your wife's name will now be Sarah instead of Sarai. I will bless her, and you will have a son by her. She will become the mother of nations, and some of her descendants will even be kings."
>
> Abraham bowed with his face to the ground and thought, "I am almost a hundred years old. How can I become a father? And Sarah is ninety. How can she have a child?" So he started laughing (Genesis 17:15-17 CEV).

Even though God's promise seemed impossible, God did have a plan, and Abraham and Sarah had to be patient while they waited for His plan to unfold. They also had to be obedient and do the things God told them to do while they waited.

Did you catch that? Being patient does not mean just sitting around and waiting for something to happen. When we have the kind of patience that comes from God, we continue to show God's love to those around us while we wait.

And of course your patience does not guarantee that things will go your way. Patience is, however, evidence that you are trusting God because you know He has a plan. God had a plan for Abraham and Sarah, He has a plan for Alena, He has a plan for me, and He has a plan for you. Things may look impossible at times, but when you choose to have patience, you are holding on to the truth that whatever God has coming will be what is best for you.

So how can you say yes to patience today?

Will you take your time while reading a book? Instead of getting frustrated, will you enjoy the people in a long line? Will you choose to enjoy being the age you are right now and patiently wait to grow up?

One way to choose to be patient is to choose to trust God. So if you're waiting to see more of God's fruit grow in your life, don't get frustrated. Instead, ask Him for help and say yes to patience.

Remember that growing the fruit of the Spirit takes time. And that's okay because we'll be loving Jesus and growing in our relationship with Him forever. I know the word "forever" can seem a little strange, but remember that forever starts today. In other words, even if something takes longer than you want it to, remember that God loves you. He started loving you long before you were born, and He will love you tomorrow and the next day and the next day...forever! And He's always ready to help you.

Let's ask Him to help us say yes to patience.

Dear God,

I am so glad to know that I will always be Your daughter and that You have good plans for me. Please help me to be patient with life the way You are patient with me. I don't want to miss the great things You have for me now or in the future. Help me to trust You as I grow and as You grow inside my heart. Help me not to be frustrated when things don't go my way, and help me to show Your love to others in every situation. I know I will make mistakes along the way, so I'm grateful You are always patient with me and ready to help me.

In Jesus's name, amen.

Sometimes when you are waiting for something to happen, it's a good idea to find something else to do. Here are a few ideas that might help the time go faster.

1. Dance.

2. Teach yourself something. It could be anything—playing an instrument, sewing a dress for a doll, decorating a cake, baking your favorite cookies, or sharpening your Photoshop skills.

3. Create a board game. Use trinkets from around your house as the pieces.

4. Organize a play. Come up with a plot, write a script, pick costumes, set the stage, and present the show to your family and friends.

5. Spend time with your family.

6. Have a photo shoot. Gather your family and some stuffed animals or other items from around your house. Then arrange people and props for some fun pictures.

7. Take a nature walk. Take pictures, collect items, and create a fun craft when you return.

8. Set up a treasure hunt. Hide fun things around your house or your neighborhood, write clues, and send your friends to find them.

9. Write a letter or note to someone.

10. Spend time with God. Read your Bible and talk to Him.

While you wait, say yes to patience.

10

Saying Yes to Kindness

Have you ever noticed that kindness is contagious? Think about a time when you were having a bad day, but then someone smiled or said something kind to you, and suddenly you felt better. Whenever that happens to me, I am grateful for the unexpected kindness—and then I want to surprise someone with my kindness.

This chain of kindness is a part of God's plan. As I've said, one reason God grows His fruit in His children is so we can share that fruit with those around us. God wants us to share the love, the joy, the peace, the patience, and—as we'll see today—the kindness. Everything God grows in us is for us to enjoy *and* to give to others.

You see, whatever God gives us doesn't actually belong to us. Everything belongs to Him, and He has chosen us to take care of all He's given us and share it with others.

When I was a little girl, my mother was always so kind to the people around her—even to strangers. She would pick up people at the bus stop and take them wherever they needed to go. When she saw older people carrying packages or walking slowly, she would help them to their cars. She would even give people money if they needed it.

I never really understood why my mom did these things. We didn't have much money ourselves. And why would we give a stranger a ride? What if that person hurt my mom or tried to steal our car? I often asked myself these questions, and I had a hard time coming up with answers.

But now I think I have answers to some of those questions. I've come to understand that my mother realized everything she had belonged to God. Of course, she was wise and only picked up people she thought looked safe. But she also believed that God would protect us.

My mother knew that God would provide her with everything she needed. She knew she didn't have to worry about taking care of herself because she trusted God to do that.

Kindness may be contagious, but being kind isn't always easy. We've seen, for instance, that we can't produce the fruit of the Spirit on our own. God grows His fruit in us by the power and presence of His Spirit. Also, being kind requires that we think of those around us instead of thinking only about ourselves, and that approach to life definitely requires help from God.

So what are some ways you show people kindness? Maybe you're resting comfortably on the couch, you hear your mom struggling with the grocery bags, and you jump up to help her even when you don't feel like it. This is the type of kindness God wants to give us through His Spirit, and He gives us a picture of this kindness in the Bible.

Have you ever heard of Ruth and Naomi? One of the Bible books in the Old Testament is called Ruth. Read it to learn more about her life and to see how kind she was because of God's kindness to her.

The Bible tells us that Ruth lived in a country called Moab and was married to a man named Mahlon. His mother and father lived nearby, as did Mahlon's brother and his wife, Orpah.

When Mahlon's father died, his mother, Naomi, continued to live near her sons and daughters-in-law. Sadly, both of Naomi's sons died, leaving the three women widowed and alone.

Naomi told Ruth and Orpah she had decided to return to the land of Israel, where she had grown up. She told her daughters-in-law to stay in Moab, their homeland.

Can you imagine how alone and sad they all must have felt? Especially Naomi. Having lost her husband and her sons, she didn't have any family left except for Ruth and Orpah. But she advised them to stay in Moab. Naomi knew that Ruth and Orpah would want to be with their families now that their husbands were gone too.

The Bible says that Orpah was sad about saying goodbye, but she eventually left Naomi and Ruth. She decided to return to her family just as Naomi had told her to. But you know what? Ruth refused to leave her mother-in-law. Naomi continued to encourage Ruth to return to her parents, but Ruth would not. Even though Naomi didn't have anything she could give Ruth, hear what Ruth told Naomi...

> Stop urging me to abandon you!
> For wherever you go, I will go.
> Wherever you live, I will live.
> Your people will become my people,
> and your God will become my God
> (Ruth 1:16 NET).

Ruth knew that Naomi didn't have anything to give her, but Ruth was kind to Naomi anyway. Ruth didn't want Naomi to be alone, and showing Naomi kindness was important to Ruth. (If you read the rest of Ruth's story in the Bible, you'll see how very, very kind God was to her.)

Sometimes it can be hard to be kind to our family and closest friends, and it can also be hard to be kind to people we don't know well. No matter how hard it is to obey, we need to do what Jesus taught us:

> Treat others in the same way that you would
> want them to treat you (Luke 6:31 NET).

In other words, do something for someone that you would want them to do for you, regardless of who they are. God doesn't say, "Be kind if someone is kind to you," does He? That assignment would be a lot easier, wouldn't it? But God wants us to be like Ruth and like my mother. He wants us to choose to be kind to people even if they have nothing to offer us and no matter how they treat us.

I know this command isn't easy to obey. But think about it this way: Does God treat you the way you treat Him? Of course not. He treats you way better than you treat Him. He shows you His kindness even though you have nothing to give back to Him.

Imagine that you and I were on the playground, and your mother walked up to me and gave me a bag of your favorite candy. I take the bag from her and run off to the swings by myself, leaving you on the other side of the playground. I sit down and quietly eat all the candy while you watch. Would you think I was being mean?

Of course you would think I was being mean—and selfish...because I was! And being selfish is the opposite of being kind. A selfish person thinks of herself more often and more highly than she thinks about anyone else, and selfish people take care of their own needs.

But you are God's girl. That means you don't have to take care of your own needs because God is taking care of you. Being God's girl also means you can share anything you have.

Remember that God showed us the greatest kindness ever when He sent His Son, Jesus, to die for our sins. The kindness you show people around you will help them to see Jesus's kindness in you.

What will you do to say yes to kindness today?

Dear God,

Thank You for being so kind. I can never say thank You enough or pay You back for all You have done for me. Help me to follow Your example and show that same kindness to others. I want to be willing to give anything I have to others because I know that everything I have was given to me by You.

In Jesus's name, amen.

Melanie Said Yes

You don't have to travel around the world to help others. You can choose to help people right in your church, neighborhood, or city. People across town and people across oceans need to know God's kindness.

My friend Melanie loves to show God's kindness to people who are homeless or hungry by giving them a "blessing bag."

A blessing bag is simply a brown lunch bag full of snacks, a bottle of water, toothpaste, soap, and a toothbrush. Melanie started doing this because of a school project when she was in the fourth grade. Her teacher gave each student $2 and told them to find a way to bless someone with the money. Melanie planned on just getting an apple and something else small to give to a homeless man in her neighborhood. However, when she arrived at the store, she found an additional $25 in the parking lot. Instead of keeping the money, she decided to add it to the $2 her teacher had given her. With $27, she was able to buy enough food to fill a few bags.

Now, years later, Melanie and her family always have a few blessing bags in their car. Whenever they see someone in need, they can reach into the back and give a bag to that person.

Melanie's family does this without asking for anything in return. They love saying yes to kindness so others will discover or at least get a glimpse of how much God loves them.

In case you're wondering, you can make blessing bags too. Get some brown lunch bags and then put whatever toiletries or food items you can fit inside, add a Scripture or a note, and ask your mom or dad if you can keep a few bags in the car.

Now think of five other ways you can show kindness to someone who has nothing to give to you.

1. _____

2. _____

3. _____

4. _____

5. _____

11

Saying Yes to Goodness

What is the first thing that comes to mind when you see the word "good"?

I think about being on my best behavior. I don't know about you, but I don't like getting into trouble. I guess you could call me a little bit of a rule follower, and that's not always a bad thing. However, God has more for us than just following rules.

Following rules, staying out of trouble, and making good choices are important. I'm sure it makes your mom happy when you behave well, and even more important, your good behavior makes God happy too. He wants His girls to shine for Him in everything we do. That means always doing our best.

But did you know that even our best is still not good enough for God? I know that sounds harsh, but it's true. The good that God wants for you and me is more than just us being on our best behavior. As you've heard me say before, God wants to make us good from the inside out. Oh, He wants to help us to do good deeds and say good words and think good thoughts, but even better, He wants our hearts to be full of and overflowing with His goodness. And God's goodness enables us to do much more than any good we could accomplish on our own.

When something is good, you want more and more of it, right? That's how it is with God's goodness in your life. His goodness makes you want more and more of Him. God's goodness makes others want Him too.

Jesus's life illustrates God's goodness. The Gospels—Matthew, Mark, Luke, and John—are full of stories about Jesus and the good things He did for people. He healed sick people, brought dead people back to life, and offered hope to everyone around Him. Jesus lived a life full of God's goodness, and His example made some people want to live that way too.

Let me explain.

When you are full of God's goodness, you want to do good things for the people around you. You don't want to see them sad or hurting. So you show them God's goodness so they will want His goodness in their lives too.

A word the Bible uses to talk about another type of goodness is "righteousness." That's a big word, but reading the first five letters will help you understand its meaning: "right." God wants to make us right. Even more than helping us to make right decisions and do right things, God wants to make us right with Him. We definitely can't do that on our own. We need God's help. We need God's Spirit to grow His right-ness inside us.

We often try to change our hearts by making sure we do the right thing, but that's not the way it works. God wants more than actions that look good; He wants us to be good on the inside. He wants our hearts to be good so that we are honest, sincere, genuine, loving, and all the good things that make us more like Jesus.

If we aren't careful, though, we can read the Bible as if it were full of rules about the countless things we should and shouldn't do. But God's rules are not the way He helps us to become more like Jesus. He doesn't give us a list of rules and then reward us with good things when we follow His commands or punish us when we don't. Instead, He wants us to love Him with our heart so that He can forgive us and we can live in relationship with Him. When we walk close to Him through our lives, He fills our days with good things that point people to His love.

Remember, anything good in us comes from God's goodness poured into our hearts; it is His love that shows up in our actions. Good things will not always be happening around you, but with God's Spirit in you, you can say yes to goodness in any circumstances.

God wants to help us focus on Him even when life is hard or when others are not good to us.

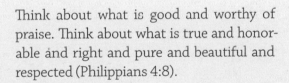

Think about what is good and worthy of praise. Think about what is true and honorable and right and pure and beautiful and respected (Philippians 4:8).

So the next time you are having a hard time seeing goodness around you, remember that you have a choice. You can choose to focus on things that are good and right. Most importantly, you can choose to reveal God's goodness as you are good to the people around you.

Dear God,

You are good. Thank You for being good all the time. I am grateful that You want to fill me with Your goodness. Please help me to focus on You regardless of what is happening around me. Teach me to "think about what is good and worthy of praise...what is true and honorable and right and pure and beautiful and respected" (Philippians 4:8) so that my words, actions, and attitudes—resulting from my thoughts—can better reflect Your goodness.

In Jesus's name, amen.

Melissa Said Yes

I am sure you have noticed that each one of us is unique. Our differences are good because all of us are created by a good Father. God has a purpose and plan for every person's life. No matter what situations and relationships may look like to us, we can focus on the truth that God's purpose and plans are always great and always intended for our good.

With that in mind, I want you to meet Melissa. She was born with spina bifida. That means her spine didn't fully develop the way it was supposed to, making some activities, like walking, difficult without assistance. Some people with this condition use walkers or crutches, but Melissa uses braces to help her walk.

Melissa refuses to let spina bifida keep her from experiencing the great life God created her to enjoy. I'll share an example. For many years, Melissa wanted to participate in a 5K race. Even though she can't run very fast, she was determined to do it.

One of her favorite Bible verses is Joshua 1:9: "Be strong and courageous...for the LORD your God will be with you wherever you go" (NIV). Melissa knows that God is always with her, and she chooses to focus on Him and His goodness.

So not long ago, Melissa participated in her first 5K. Since then she has participated in at least 30 other races. In fact, instead of having a birthday party every year, she organizes and hosts her own race! And instead of collecting presents for herself, she asks every participant to bring presents to give to other children. She collects things like soap, washcloths, school supplies, shoes, clothes, and toys.

Melissa and her entire family love to make a difference in the world by letting others see and experience God's goodness. Regardless of the challenges she faces, Melissa loves to encourage and inspire others to try hard things and to have faith that God will be right there with them.

Regardless of what is happening in your life, don't let anything keep you from showing others how good God is.

12

Saying Yes to Faithfulness

Living as God's girl leads to adventure and wonderful experiences. When you follow God, you never know where He will take you, but you can trust that it will always be for your good.

> Trust the LORD completely, and don't depend on your own knowledge. With every step you take, think about what he wants, and he will help you go the right way (Proverbs 3:5-6).

Following God can sometimes feel like you're living in a mystery. He rarely tells us what tomorrow will bring. After all, He wants us to continue to trust Him and be confident that He is leading us somewhere great.

Following God takes faith. Having faith means you believe something is true even when you can't see it or understand it. Faith also means not only *saying* you believe something, but also *acting* like you believe.

Our faith can grow stronger when we remind ourselves that God loves taking care of us. He loves surprising all His children with experiences and opportunities that help us better understand how much He loves us. Our job is to trust and believe that what He says is true and to make choices that show others how much we trust Him.

Think about it this way...

Do you ever worry about having air to breathe? You probably don't even think about it. You just inhale and exhale all day long, every single day, and you never doubt that air will continue to be available to you and continue to do what it needs to do in your body.

We can have this same confidence about God. Every day He wants us to live for Him even though we can't see Him or see what He is doing. God wants us to trust that He is always available to us and that He is doing what He needs to do in our hearts and in our lives. Because He is!

And now it's time for me to admit something to you.

Ready?

Here it is: I am not a big fan of surprises. I always like to know exactly what is going on. This makes it a little hard for me to trust God when I don't know what's ahead—which is quite often!

When I was little, my mother loved planning fun things for my brother and me. We never knew what her plans for us were or when they would happen. One time, for example, she woke up my brother and me on a Saturday morning and told us to get dressed, pack a bag, and hop in the car. Having absolutely no idea where we were headed, my brother and I complained a little about having to get up. Our beds were warm and comfortable—and it was the weekend! We really wanted to sleep, but we (not very happily) did what we were told. We wiped the sleep from our eyes, slid out of our beds, and begged Mom to tell us where we were going.

She refused. She simply teased us with a smile and a few giggles. "You'll see," she told us. "Just do what I asked you to do."

With her continued motivation, we did our best to follow her directions because she assured us that something great was ahead. We didn't understand why she woke us up, and we didn't know all the plans and details. But we trusted our mother, so we knew our obedience would lead to something great. We just couldn't wait to find out what it was. So we hurriedly brushed our teeth, put on a pair of jeans and a T-shirt, stuffed a few random items into an overnight bag, and headed for the car.

We drove for what felt like days (it was really only a few hours), and we finally ended up in New York City! (I grew up in Baltimore, Maryland, so New York was not too far away.) My mother had an aunt and a few cousins who lived there, so it was the perfect place to visit.

Going to New York was always an adventure, and that weekend was no exception. What started out as a normal day ended with us eating fun treats and strolling through the streets of a different city with our family. My brother and I were so glad our mother loved us enough to plan such a fun surprise. We were also very glad that even when we complained about having to wake up so early on a weekend, and even when we moaned about the long car ride, she didn't change her plans for us.

I wish I could tell you that after our New York adventure, I always did exactly what my mother said to do because I knew my obedience would lead to something great. But unfortunately, I can't. Sometimes my mother woke me up and gave me clear instructions to follow, but I complained because she was interrupting my comfort or sleep. Other times I even worried that the mysterious adventure she was planning wouldn't be fun, and I wished she would let me plan my day myself.

But do you know what? My bad attitude and my slowness to follow directions never stopped my mother from planning great things for me. Even as my brother and I got older, she continued to give us great experiences and plan adventures that were both fun and important for our lives. I admit, sometimes I didn't enjoy them as much as I could have because I was too busy complaining or wishing I were doing something else.

I'm telling you this because—you guessed it!—sometimes I even do this with God. I worry because I want to know what He has planned for me. I complain because He is asking me to do things I don't want to do. But the truth is, God knows exactly what He is doing in my life. I just need to choose to have faith in Him and to be faithful in my actions and my love for Him.

Trusting that someone else knows what is best for you can be really hard. That's why God wants to help us.

You see, faithfulness is another fruit of the Spirit that God grows in His children. The more we follow Him, the more faithful to Him we become. God wants us to trust Him, and trust means doing the things He tells us to do. When we are faithful to obey and follow God, people around us can see how much we trust Him and will be likely to get a glimpse of His irresistible, life-giving love.

Dear God,

I am so glad I can trust You. I know that You have a wonderful adventure planned for my life, and I want to enjoy all of it. Help me to do the things You ask me to do even when I don't understand everything about the command or know anything about the future. Help me to have faith in You and to be faithful to You.

In Jesus's name, amen.

Be Faithful—God Has a Plan

"I know the plans that I have for you." This message is from the LORD. "I have good plans for you. I don't plan to hurt you. I plan to give you hope and a good future" (Jeremiah 29:11).

I love reading this verse because it reminds me that God has good plans for us. But did you know that when God first gave this message to His people, the Israelites, a lot of not-so-good things were happening?

During this time, the Israelites were exiles living where they did not want to live. They had been forced to leave their home in Jerusalem and were being held captive in Babylon, a place that was nothing like their home. Furthermore, the Israelites were not always treated well by the Babylonians.

From the Israelites' point of view, it sure didn't look like God had a plan—especially not a good plan. But He did. God wanted His people to learn to trust Him even though they were going through difficult circumstances.

He even told them to pray for the people around them and to serve and help in the city where they were forced to live. (You may know how hard it is to pray for people who are mean to you!) In other words, God wanted the Israelites to remember their relationship with Him even when they couldn't see good things happening around them. God wanted His people to be faithful to Him even when life was hard and His ways were puzzling.

God wants us to be faithful too. He wants our relationship with Him to be the most important thing in our lives even when nothing around us seems good.

When everything in life is going well and we're feeling happy, it's a little easier to trust that God has a good plan for us. However, when things are hard and we're sad or frustrated or worried, we can forget or even stop believing that God actually has a good plan for us. When people are being mean to us, when we can't seem to get good grades, or when we don't think our parents understand, it becomes really tempting to stop trusting God and instead take charge of our lives. But God wants us to continue to trust Him and to continue to follow Him...because He has a plan.

As the plan unfolds mysteriously and sometimes slowly, remember that God always wants you to talk to Him and to ask Him for any help you need. Even though God has good plans for you, your life will sometimes be hard. Realize that God uses every situation—the good ones as well as the not-so-great ones and the totally hard times too—in His good plan for your life.

13

Saying Yes to Gentleness

L et's play a game.
I'll say a word, and you think of the opposite. Okay?

Run _____

Fun _____

Asleep _____

I'm sure it wasn't hard for you to come up with opposites for those words.

But why did I ask you to do this? Because one way to understand what a word means is to consider what it does *not* mean.

I think "gentle" is one of those words.

Before we try to define "gentle," let's look at two of its opposites: "harsh" and "severe." Hold that thought!

Now, we may think that being gentle means not having any strength or being weak, but that is not what "gentle" means at all. "Gentle" means that we do not use all the strength that we have because we are being considerate of someone or something else.

For example, we are gentle with babies because we don't want to hurt them or frighten them. We are bigger and stronger; they are delicate and fragile. So we touch babies carefully and use a calm, soft voice when we talk to them.

Have you ever watched a daddy holding his tiny baby? Even though he is big and strong, he chooses not to use all his strength when he holds the child. When he hugs his baby, he is careful not to squeeze too tightly. The baby's experience is more important to Daddy than his own.

To be gentle, we have to understand someone else's needs. That requires thoughtfulness and consideration, which call for a different kind of strength than big muscles or a loud voice. Being gentle requires power that neither you nor I can adequately have on our own. To be sufficiently and appropriately gentle, we need to rely on God's Spirit to grow His fruit inside us.

You see, when we choose to let God's gentle Spirit live inside us and work through us, people around us can see His presence in us, and those observers often want to know more about the gentle God we love. These observers will also appreciate you, knowing from your gentleness that you are thinking about them and their needs.

Jesus is the perfect example of gentleness. The Bible even describes Him that way.

> Take my yoke on you and learn from me, because I am gentle and humble in heart, and you will find rest for your souls (Matthew 11:29 NET).

Let's get one thing straight—Jesus is not weak. Not at all! Some people were cruel to Him. They called Him names, treated Him terribly, and plotted against Him as if He were a criminal. And Jesus was absolutely strong enough to stop the abuse if He had wanted to. (Of course Jesus didn't like the cruelty, but He was choosing to do what God wanted Him to do. This was part of God's ultimately good plan for Jesus—and for you and me.) Jesus didn't have to show these cruel people love, and He doesn't have to show you and me love either. And yet He did and He does!

Jesus's gentle spirit also allowed Him to put up with all the cruel things that others did and said to Him. And because of His love for them, He chose to endure the difficult moments so He could follow through on God's plan to save mankind from their sin. If He had not chosen gentleness but had opted to be harsh or severe, He might have allowed us to suffer the consequences we deserve for our sin. In fact, our holy God would have been forced to punish us for our bad decisions.

We see Jesus's gentleness in His willingness to die for us. The cross is an important reminder that God chose to be gentle with us...and that choice meant watching His Son die on the cross.

> He was treated badly, but he never protested. He said nothing, like a lamb being led away to be killed. He was like a sheep that makes no sound as its wool is being cut off. He never opened his mouth to defend himself. He was taken away by force and judged unfairly...But he was put to death for the sins of his people (Isaiah 53:7-8).

Jesus chose to be humble and gentle. He never fought back when people were cruel to Him. He cared about us enough to die for us.

So, how can you be gentle today? Who can you show that you care about them and their welfare? Decide now when and where will you demonstrate Christlike gentleness today—and remember that God will help you.

Dear God,

Thank You for Jesus's example of gentleness. Thank You for giving me enough strength to *not* do everything I want to do or could do in a difficult situation. Please help me to be gentle with my words and my actions when it would be easier to be harsh. Help me to be calm and kind. Thank You that I can rely on You for everything, just as a baby relies on his or her parent. I want Your gentleness to be obvious in me when everyone thinks I should be cruel; I want to rest when others think I should fight back. Please continue to grow Your gentleness in me. Thank You.

In Jesus's name, amen.

My Mother Said Yes

My mother is one of the gentlest people I know. She is also really strong.

My mother loves people. She loves talking to them, helping them, and getting to know things about their lives. Most people love her because she is so nice and thoughtful. She cares about their needs and will do anything she can to help them. In fact, I sometimes got upset because she always chose to say and do nice things. I didn't understand how she could do that all the time. I am sure she had her bad days—I just don't remember them!

One day when I asked her why she was nice to everyone, she told me a story that explained everything. She had a coworker who, for whatever reason, chose to be very unkind to my mother. She said mean things about my mother to the other people at work, and she even told my mother how much she didn't like her. No one knew why this coworker acted this way, but her behavior did not keep my mother from being kind to her.

Now, let me be honest. Sometimes when someone is mean to me or makes it clear she doesn't like me, I can much too easily say mean things back or at least ignore the person. Well, my mother chose not to do either of those things. Instead, the meaner this woman was, the nicer my mother was. She chose to use kind words and to be gentle.

Aware that her coworker did not know God, my mother knew that God wanted her to be gentle and kind so that God could show Himself to the coworker through my mother. Throughout the long time this woman chose to be rude, my mother continued to treat her coworker with gentleness.

One day this woman needed a ride home from work, and my mother offered to drive her. Her coworker could not understand why my mother had never spoken harshly to her, and she certainly couldn't understand why my mother would offer her a ride home! She was confused by my mother's soft demeanor—to say the least.

This drive home and her coworker's puzzlement gave my mother the chance to tell her about God's love and grace. My mother told this woman about how loving, kind, and gentle God is with us even when we are harsh or mean to Him.

And you probably can guess what happened next.

This woman became a very close friend to my mother and to Jesus. Yes, she started to live for Jesus too.

> A gentle response turns away anger,
> but a harsh word stirs up wrath
> (Proverbs 15:1 NET).

My mother knew this truth from God's Word, and she had seen gentleness turn away anger in her own life. This experience with her coworker was clearly one of those times. The Holy Spirit gave my mother the power to show a cruel person the gentleness and love of God. He used the fruit of gentleness evident in my mother to get her coworker's attention. That woman came to know God, and now she is an example of God's power, fruit, and love.

This woman's heart and life were changed because my mother was willing to say yes to God, to say yes to gentleness. How awesome is that!

14

Saying Yes to Self-Control

Wen you hear the word "self-control," what comes to mind? What pictures or thoughts pop into your head? When I hear the word "self-control," I immediately think of discipline and hard work and rules. For most of my life, especially as a little girl, I thought more about the things I *shouldn't* do than the things I *could* do and *should* do.

For example, in the home where I grew up, listening to music that wasn't specifically *Christian* music was a no-no.

I also knew where I couldn't go in the big city where we lived. I was not allowed to go past one particular crack in the sidewalk to the right of our porch, and I couldn't cross the street in the other direction.

I knew I wasn't supposed to use bad words, hang out with the wrong people, or talk back to my mother.

I guess you could say I was trained that way. So knowing what I shouldn't do seemed very natural to me. Just like breathing.

But to be honest with you, I was annoyed by these rules even when I was a little girl. I had lots of friends who were allowed to listen to other kinds of music. Why couldn't I?

And I had lots of friends who could wander the city. Why did my mom have to be so strict?

When I was young, these ways I was different from my friends made me think a lot of negative thoughts that probably weren't healthy for me. I believed that most of these rules were unfair and that they seemed to follow me wherever I went.

But now I know that these rules weren't necessarily bad. Most of them were good, and I give my daughters similar rules today.

I didn't know at the time that my mother was trying to keep me safe and teach me self-control.

My mother knew what it was like to say yes to God in every part of her life, and she was doing her best to teach me to do the same. Some of the rules she established were small ways to help me understand the difference between saying yes to God and saying yes to what everyone else thought I should do.

Some of the reasons God gives us rules are the same reasons my mother gave me rules. God wants us safe, He wants us to be wise, and He wants to train us to say yes to Him. He knows that being under control is a good thing. In fact, it's a God thing.

Think about your favorite amusement park ride. Would you get on that ride if no one was making sure it worked properly?

I don't like scary rides myself, but my little girls love them. I let them get on rides—but only when I know an operator is making sure everything is working properly.

And all amusement park rides have operators, and all rides have rules. You have to have both in order to have a good experience. This is true for life as well. We need someone watching over us: God is like the ride operator of our lives. And we need some instruction, so God has given us the Bible, which is way better than a list of rules.

But here's one way that our lives are different from an amusement park ride. Imagine that the operator of a ride invited you to help him with the controls. Wouldn't that be awesome!

Well, that's basically what God has done in our lives. He has given us the incredible responsibility and privilege of operating the ride—with His help and guidance.

You and I both know that a ride wouldn't be fun if all we could do was look at the rules and see a list of things we *couldn't* do. Imagine standing in front of your favorite roller coaster, wanting to join the fun...but then reading a sign that says you are too short to get on. That would be so disappointing. Now imagine going back to the ride a year later and a few inches taller, excited about finally being able to join your friends on the ride...but you see another sign that says the cost of the ride has gone way up, and you don't have enough money. How sad would that be!

Imagine going back every year, and each time finding a list of rules telling you what you *can't* do. What a nightmare!

Well, I'm so glad to tell you that your life with God is not like that.

Yes, He gives you "rules"—the Bible, which includes helpful instructions on how to enjoy your life with Him. And yes, He knows you need an operator—the Holy Spirit, whom God has sent to live in you. God gives you His Word and His Spirit so you don't have to stand in line and watch life happen. He wants you to be an active participant, to enjoy "the ride of life" side by side with Him.

One of God's goals for your life is for you to get better and better and better at following His instructions and operating your life in a way that pleases Him and benefits others.

God doesn't want you to live your life saying no to things. Nope. Remember the title of this book? He wants you to be a girl who knows how to say yes to Him and to the adventure He has invited you to enjoy.

You see, in Jesus and through the Holy Spirit, God has given us the freedom and the power to say yes to Him and to His plan for us. At times that requires saying no to other things so we can choose God's way.

And *that* is what self-control is. It is saying yes to God and His way and saying no to anything that takes us in the wrong direction.

Does saying yes to God—and no to the other option—sometimes seem impossible? Absolutely! Saying yes to God is hard for all of us. In fact, sometimes it's impossible! Even Jesus bumped up against the seemingly impossible. He wrestled in prayer before His death; He struggled and asked to avoid the path to the cross God had for Him.

But guess what? Jesus surrendered His will and said yes to God. He is our perfect example of self-control even when His yes to God meant His death. We read in the book of Hebrews that Jesus lived a life of complete self-control.

> This High Priest of ours understands our weaknesses, for he faced all of the same testings we do, yet he did not sin (Hebrews 4:15 NLT).

Jesus never once sinned. You know why? Because He was God.

How does that help you and me? We don't always say yes to God the way Jesus did. Actually, that's the best part! Through the Holy Spirit, God gives you and me the ability to say yes to Him—just as Jesus said yes.

> If the Spirit of him who raised Jesus from the dead dwells in you, he who raised Christ Jesus from the dead will also give life to your mortal bodies through his Spirit who dwells in you (Romans 8:11 ESV).

When I was a little girl, I didn't understand some things about the rules God has given us. But here are two lessons I've learned since then, and the first is the more important one.

- God gave us more than rules—He also gave us a relationship with Him. As I grew up, my mom was able to explain to me why her rules were good. In the same way, as we practice saying yes to God, He helps us to understand more about the things He tells us in His Word.

- Our life is not about rules. It's actually about being free to live an amazing adventure with God. Like the amusement park ride, we need some rules to help us know how to avoid hurting ourselves. Also like the ride, we have a trustworthy operator. But of course God isn't like any other operator. He knows everything, He can do anything, and He invites us to handle the controls and operate our life with Him. Through His Spirit working inside of us, He gives us power to say yes to all that He has for us.

I love to eat. Do you?

Because I love to eat, sometimes it's really hard for me to share. In fact, I once had an argument with my best friend over a box of donuts. Here's what happened...

A new donut shop opened up an hour away from where we lived. We decided to take a special drive to get some. When we arrived, we ate a few donuts, and then I decided to get a box to take home with me. I wanted to have them in the morning for breakfast.

But guess what my friend did? That's right—he asked for one of my donuts. He thought that because I had an entire box, I wouldn't mind giving him another one. I was very upset...but later, I was so embarrassed by my decision. I only thought about *my* needs and what *I* wanted. The Holy Spirit would have wanted me to share, but I chose my own way. Instead of saying yes to loving with God's love, I said no.

My lack of self-control ruined the donuts for me, and my selfish choice hurt my relationship with my best friend. To be honest, the donuts weren't even that good after that. My choice didn't please God, and it wasn't helpful for me or my best friend.

Often when the Bible teaches us about self-control, it mentions our stomachs and our appetites. That works for me because I love to talk about food!

Eating something delicious makes my stomach happy, and it makes me happy too. Unfortunately, most of my favorite things to eat (like donuts!) really are not good for me at all. Especially not when I want to eat an entire box of them. I love to eat things like brownies, candy bars, and ice cream. My all-time favorite ice cream is chocolate chip cookie dough. What's yours?

Treats like these may be delicious, but if I eat too much of them, I may end up with an upset stomach, a toothache, or even an illness. There is nothing wrong with having a brownie, but sometimes I want to eat an entire pan! Of course that wouldn't be good for me. But sometimes I enjoy my snacks so much, I don't even realize how much I've eaten until my stomach starts to hurt. Knowing when I've had enough requires a lot of self-control, and saying no to another bite is not easy for me. Not at all.

For our own good, God wants you and me to have self control. That means knowing when we have had enough of something and when we need to stop. Maybe you don't like the same snacks I do, and you have no problem saying no to those. That's great! But I'm pretty sure you *do* have a hard time saying no to something else. Could it be saying no to...

- Speaking words that might upset a friend?
- Thinking thoughts that don't make you feel good?
- Participating in activities that might sound fun but could be harmful?
- Limiting social media and computer time?

If you need help knowing when to stop, you are not alone. Sometimes our bodies, our minds, or our emotions want to be in charge, but they don't have to be. Help is available.

Having self-control is hard, and that's why it is one fruit of the Spirit that God wants you to grow in you.

God knows that it is much easier to do what you enjoy. But He also knows that fun things (eating an entire box of donuts) can hurt us if we're not careful.

When God chose you and me, He wanted our lives to be different from the lives of the people around us. He doesn't want us to continue doing whatever makes us feel good without thinking about the effects of those choices on us and on others.

Self-control is all about making the God choice. You get to make a lot of choices every day, but in each situation you have only two options: You can say yes to God, or you can say no to Him.

In the Bible, God shares the very best way for us to live with self-control.

> That is the way we should live, because God's grace has come. That grace can save everyone. It teaches us not to live against God and not to do the bad things the world wants to do. It teaches us to live on earth now in a wise and right way—a way that shows true devotion to God (Titus 2:11-12).

God wants to make sure that you want Him more than anything else. You can absolutely have too many donuts, but you can never have too much of God's sweet Spirit.

Dear God,

Thank You for reminding me that life is best lived when it's under control. Under Your control. And thank You that when I give You control, You are not selfish with me. You provide everything I need, and I never have to worry. Thank You for growing me up and teaching me to live with self-control, a fruit of Your Spirit. Lord, help me to exercise self-control. May Your power and Your Spirit working inside me help me to operate my life in a way that helps others to see how good life with You can be.

In Jesus's name, amen.

15

Let's Dream

I don't know about you, but talking about the fruit of the Spirit has made me hungry!

But wait. I'm not hungry for an apple—I'm hungry for more of God. The more I learn about saying yes to God and about the amazing things He does when His Spirit grows in our hearts, the more excited I get about being His child and walking with Him every day of my life.

And God gets excited too. He loves having relationships with His children, and as He teaches in the Bible, we need to stay close to Him in order to survive.

> I am the vine, and you are the branches. If you stay joined to me, and I to you, you will produce plenty of fruit. But separated from me you won't be able to do anything (John 15:5).

The fruit of the Spirit will grow inside of you as you stay connected to God.

What can you do to stay connected to God? Here are three of the most important ways:

1. *Reading your Bible* every day is a great way to get to know God—and get to know Him better. No one knows what Jesus's face looks like, but the words in the Bible give us a picture of His love. Each book of the Bible is full of true stories that help us see inside God's heart.

2. Spending time with God also means *praying*, and praying is simply having a conversation with God. You don't have to use big words or think of fancy things to say. You can talk to God respectfully, kindly, and pretty much just like you talk to your friends. And we read in the Bible that we should pray all the time.

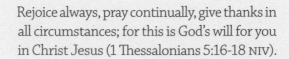

> Rejoice always, pray continually, give thanks in all circumstances; for this is God's will for you in Christ Jesus (1 Thessalonians 5:16-18 NIV).

One more thing. When you pray, remember that praying is not only you talking to God. God wants to talk to you too. Be sure to leave quiet space in your conversations so He can speak to your heart.

3. Another great way to stay connected to God is to *sing worship songs, praise Him, and thank Him*. God loves to hear His children worship Him, and our thankfulness brings us closer to Him.

> Come through the gates to his Temple
> giving thanks to him.
> Enter his courtyards with songs of praise.
> Honor him and bless his name
> (Psalm 100:4).

Always be willing to praise God, no matter what is happening in your life. Sometimes things will happen that make you feel as if God is far away, but don't ever believe that. God is always close by, and He is always ready to listen.

I have talked a lot, haven't I? That's because—as I mentioned at the very beginning—I had so much I wanted to tell you. I normally don't talk this much, so I'm glad you are still here!

In fact, I'm actually a pretty quiet person. I have been told that I'm a great friend to have in a group because I really prefer not to complicate things too much. I like to help keep things calm and peaceful.

If, for example, I'm with a group of people and they decide they want to grab a pizza, watch a certain movie, play a game, or go to a store, I'll easily agree. I don't do that because I like to make them happy or because I'm afraid to say what I really want, but normally their choices honestly don't bother me, so I'm happy to go along with whatever has been decided.

But sometimes that's not how I feel. Every once in a while, I really want to do a certain thing. I have a plan or an idea that I think is great, and I know exactly how I want it to happen. Usually my friends are excited and eager to do something my way because they know it must really mean a lot to me if I've spoken up. However, sometimes in the middle of my plans, they forget that what we are doing was actually my idea. They don't mean to take over, but little by little they start to do things their way. And before I know it, nothing is happening the way I had imagined.

Has that ever happened to you?

Maybe you planned a sleepover, and you knew exactly how you wanted it to go. You invited your friends, made the schedule, chose the menu, and got ready for all the activities. But when everyone showed up, they didn't want to watch the movie you'd chosen, eat the snacks you had ready, or do the activities you'd prepared. Your friends probably thought they were helping to make your sleepover better, but you were more than a little sad because you had pictured how things would be, and you thought your plan was great!

Well, friend, I think this issue of plans, expectations, and control can also be an issue in our relationship with God.

Our plans, our expectations, and our control won't be issues if we remember that our lives are God's idea and that He had our paths planned out before were born.

> God planned long ago to choose you and to make you his holy people, which is the Spirit's work. God wanted you to obey him and to be made clean by the blood sacrifice of Jesus Christ (1 Peter 1:2).

The word "holy" can seem a little scary, but it doesn't have to be. "Holy" simply means "unique, special, and set apart." God calls us His holy people because He has set us apart from people who don't say yes to Him. We are special to Him because we have chosen to say yes. And He who created you as one of a kind has a unique and special life planned for you. To help you navigate life, God sent His Holy Spirit to—among other things—lead you, teach you, and comfort you.

But sometimes, like the friend who tries to be in charge at your sleepover, you and I try to take control of our lives. I've done this to God before, and I didn't even realize I was doing it. I just thought I had the best idea and was making my life better.

Remember the life I dreamed I would have when I grew up? Nice house, fancy clothes, great job...I worked really hard to make that life happen. Instead of letting God's Spirit lead me, I kept making my own decisions, going the direction I wanted, trying new jobs, and, basically, doing what I saw other people doing. I did all this without asking God for any help.

Nothing is wrong with planning and dreaming and setting goals for what you want to accomplish. You can dream big with God because God really does want to do incredible things in your life. But remember that you are God's idea. So stay close to Him and always be willing to go in the direction He is leading you.

God wants us to remember that we are His chosen daughters and that the plans He has for our lives are perfect. We can follow His Spirit's guidance, trusting Him to lead us where He wants us to go. And whatever your dream, always be willing to make changes in order to do things God's way.

Would you believe me if I told you I wrote my first book when I was only seven years old? Okay, no one published it or even read it (except my mom), but it still counts. I had no idea that God's plan for my life included writing books. I just loved to write, so I did it often.

I collected a few pieces of white paper, wrote a little bit of the story on each page, added a few pictures, and stapled them together. Of course, I put the title and my name on the front, and then I gave it to my uncle. I was so proud of my book.

I didn't know whether anyone would read it. I wrote my book simply because I liked to write. I had no idea I'd one day be writing books for God, but He knew from the very beginning what He wanted me to do. God always has a plan, and He wants us to trust Him and to let His Spirit lead us into that plan.

God doesn't want us to be in charge of our lives, but nothing is wrong with dreaming big with Him. And dream big about doing for Him things you enjoy doing. I never thought God would use my love for writing stories. I just knew I liked to write. Now I get to write books and tell others about God's love.

Your combination of gifts and talents is unique to you, so don't waste time and energy comparing yourself with other people. Instead, think about which of your skills and loves God wants you to use for Him. Often—and this has been my experience—the very things we enjoy doing are the things God wants us to do to serve Him!

Maybe you love to write, sing, braid hair, or even cook. Saying yes to God means using the gifts He has given you to help those around you.

> God has shown you his grace in many different ways. So be good servants and use whatever gift he has given you in a way that will best serve each other. If your gift is speaking, your words should be like words from God. If your gift is serving, you should serve with the strength that God gives. Then it is God who will be praised in everything through Jesus Christ. Power and glory belong to him forever and ever. Amen (1 Peter 4:10-11).

I have a friend named Remmi. When Remmi was only 12 years old, she realized how much she loved to cook. She began creating easy and fun meals for her family and some of her friends. Well, guess what? Now, years later, Remmi is a chef. She even has her own television show to teach other kids how to cook. She has received awards, she helps schools create healthy meals for their students, and she wrote a cookbook.

When Remmi first starting cooking, she had no idea how many other people would benefit from her gift. She simply loved doing it! Step-by-step God showed her what He wanted her to do with her love for cooking.

Maybe you have a few dreams you enjoy thinking about—or maybe you don't, and that's okay too. When you don't know for sure what God is asking you to do, here are few good questions to ask yourself.

- Will I be showing someone love?
- Will I make someone smile?
- Will my words help someone?
- Will I be using some of my talents?
- Will I be doing something I love to do?
- Will I have a chance to share God's love or maybe even tell someone about Jesus?

Remember, God has plans that we don't know anything about—yet. He's always working behind the scenes, guiding us and leading us down His path for us.

So be ready.

I wish I could give you a perfect formula that would lead to amazing things happening in your life, but no such formula exists. All day long, you are making choices. (Remember how many?) And each choice leads to the next choice...which leads to the next one, and so on. When you keep saying yes to the opportunities God gives you, you'll eventually see the great plans He has for you unfold in your life.

Here are a few ways you can be ready to take the next step.

Seek

Think about when you've played hide-and-seek. What was the perfect hiding place that made you have to search and search and search to find your friend? Well, God isn't hiding from you. In fact, He very much wants you to find Him! So be sure to search every day for what He wants you to say yes to. Seek to make your relationship with Him the most important part of your life, the most important part of your day. You see, God wants to be with you, and He wants you to want to be with Him. And when you want to be with Him, you will see more and more evidence of His being with you.

> Above all pursue his kingdom and righteousness, and all these things will be given to you as well (Matthew 6:33 NET).

Obey

Remember that with God, obedience is all about love. We show God that we love Him when we obey Him, and we want to obey Him because we love Him.

> If you love me, you will keep my commandments (John 14:15 ESV).

Be Faithful

God hardly ever does exactly what we want Him to do at the exact moment we want Him to do it. But God's timing is perfect, and ours rarely is. When we don't see God acting the way we expect or want, we can always trust that He is doing something. So be faithful. And as your faith in Him continues to grow, you will find yourself more willing to wait for Him and to follow His directions. Again, the kind of faithfulness that God grows in your heart will help you to wait for Him. When we don't wait...when we try to do things our way...well, there is nothing amazing about that path.

> Stand firm and don't be shaken. Always keep busy working for the LORD. You know that everything you do for him is worthwhile (1 Corinthians 15:58 CEV).

It is so fun to dream. But remember that you don't have to sit around waiting for that something big you're dreaming about to happen. God has already chosen you for a special plan He designed especially for you, and His Spirit lives inside you to help you walk with God and live in a way that pleases Him. So you can just focus on following God one step at a time.

Now, take some time to think about your special talents and things you enjoy doing. List some below. You never know...God may want to use one or more of these in the wonderful plan He has for your life.

1. _____

2. _____

3. _____

4. _____

5. _____

Dear God,

Thank You for loving me and caring about me so much. I know I can trust everything You do and can confidently follow the steps You have for me because You love me. I also know that You have given me some special gifts and talents. Some of them I already know about, and some of them You may not have even shown me yet. I know You want me to use every one of my gifts to show other people Your love. Please help me to trust You and to follow You day by day. Help me become more aware of You in my days so I can follow Your leading into the life You want me to have. I know You have amazing things planned for me to do for You, and I can't wait to discover them!

In Jesus's name, amen.

Ready to Read Your Bible? Start Here.

I could tell you many more stories about people I know who have said yes to God. You can also find lots of stories like that in the Bible. Here are a few of my favorite stories about people who said yes to God.

- Peter walked on water (Matthew 14:22-33).

- David destroyed a giant with a slingshot (1 Samuel 17).

- Esther became a queen. (Read the whole book of Esther—it's short.)

- Daniel survived a night with lions (Daniel 6).

Reading these amazing accounts will encourage you to follow God on your own journey.

16

Your Turn

L et me ask you a question. Are you ready?

Okay, be honest...

Does saying yes to God scare you a little? As we've talked about, when you say yes to God, you may have to say no to some other things, right?

When I read about Katherine and Isabelle, Andy and Andrea, Melissa, Ruth, Hannah, and so many other people in the Bible and around the world, I wonder if they ever felt like saying no.

I know, I know...that possibility may surprise you, but the reality is, saying yes all the time can be hard. I wonder if Katherine and Isabelle ever want to take a nap instead of finishing a special origami design they are working on. Or maybe sometimes Remmi would rather not cook even when she knows she has to.

Sometimes I have a really hard time doing what I know I need to do.

For example, in the morning when my alarm goes off, I know I need to get up and get dressed. I know I have to be somewhere at a certain time, and I know I'll be late if I don't move quickly. Even though I know all these things, sometimes I hit the snooze button over and over again and simply don't do what I know I need to do.

Choosing to stay in bed may feel good for a little while. Snuggling under my favorite blanket is so comfortable. Clearly, sleeping a little longer is an easy choice to make.

But soon I realize what a mistake I've made, and I jump out of bed. I end up rushing, missing breakfast, and—I'm sad to admit—not being very nice to people because I'm in a hurry. But even then it's not too late for me to choose to do everything else I had planned for the day. The day didn't stop happening because of my mistake, but I would have enjoyed it more if I had made a better choice in the morning.

So you see, this is what happens when we choose to say no or not do something that we know we should. We all make mistakes. God knows that, but He *always* helps us, forgives us, and loves us—no matter what. Regardless of the mistakes we make, God never stops loving us, and His plans for us will always happen. But if we want to fully enjoy a relationship with Him, we need to learn to say yes to Him more and more.

A man's heart plans his way,
but the LORD determines his steps
(Proverbs 16:9 HCSB).

This verse does not mean that you are free to do whatever you want and expect God to make a situation all better if it goes sideways. Rather, this verse assures you that because you are God's daughter, He will continue to guide you in the direction that is best for you. He will continue to walk beside you and hear you when you pray. That's a wonderful promise for those of us who sometimes make poor decisions. And that's all of us. And that "all" includes a man named Jonah.

Have you ever heard of Jonah? A book in the Bible is named after him—but not because he was so great. Jonah blew it big-time when he said no to what God asked him to do. Jonah loved God, but he disobeyed.

If you read the entire story (it's only four short chapters), you'll discover that God told Jonah to go a city called Nineveh, a place Jonah absolutely did not want to visit even to do God's work. Maybe God's job for Jonah sounded too big and too difficult. After all, the people in Nineveh were wicked, and Jonah might have feared for his life. He also may have thought that the evil citizens of Nineveh deserved God's judgment, not a message about His forgiveness and love. Whatever his reasons, Jonah chose to do things his way, not God's way, and he jumped onto a boat that was going in the completely opposite direction.

And do you know what happened?

Jonah ended up in the belly of a fish! That's right. Jonah disobeyed God. If one reason for his disobedience was his fear of the Ninevites, Jonah found himself in a way scarier situation. But even then, God protected disobedient Jonah: He allowed Jonah to get out of the fish, and He gave Jonah a second chance to obey Him.

The story of Jonah has everything to do with God and His amazing love for His disobedient prophet and for the evil people of Nineveh.

And God's love hasn't changed. Like people in the Bible, we can be afraid to go where God tells us to go, we make mistakes, and we don't always make the best choices. Yet, just as God did amazing things in the lives of His people in the Bible, He still chooses to do amazing things in our lives.

And God will always do whatever He needs to do in order to show you how much He loves you.

Not long ago, my daughter Alena and I were invited on a trip to Israel. This sounded like an amazing opportunity, but a lot of things about the trip made me a little afraid. I kept thinking about how long the flight would be. I also wasn't sure if the country would be safe. I was so afraid, I almost didn't go.

Thankfully, Alena was not at all afraid. She was excited. She reminded me that the opportunity to take the trip was a gift from God. When she said those words, she helped me to say yes to going and no to my fears.

And I am so glad we went. While we were there, we saw many places the Bible talks about. We also met many wonderful people, and—best of all—we got to walk along many of the same roads Jesus walked on. That was amazing!

Even though Jesus lived there 2,000 years ago, I still felt that by stepping out of my comfort zone and taking the trip, I was following the footsteps of Jesus in real life. I knew that as long as I was going where He wanted me to go, I was headed in the right direction. Walking on roads in Israel where Jesus had actually left His footprints changed my life. Picturing Jesus talking to people and helping those around Him as He walked along made Him more real to me than ever before, and I became more committed to following Jesus.

> We get our new life from the Spirit, so we should follow the Spirit (Galatians 5:25).

Following the Spirit changes us. As the Spirit works in our hearts, He makes us more like Jesus. He also changes the way we see people and the way we experience life. I have definitely seen Him work in the lives of the special people I've introduced you to.

I am so grateful for Alena, who wasn't afraid to try out for a part in a movie or to hop on a plane to Israel.

I am grateful for my friends who help people get clean water.

I am so grateful for my mother and the ways she chose to show kindness to people around her. Even unkind people.

(Wow, we sure have talked about a lot!)

I am also grateful for you. Thank you for deciding to read this book. I believe that God will use something you've read to help you grow closer to Him. I also believe He is going to take you on an amazing adventure with Him. An adventure that will show others how great He is.

God uses everyone who says yes to Him.

Before I leave, I want to take a minute and let you talk some too. I think now is a great time!

What have you enjoyed most while learning about my friends as well as people from the Bible and around the world?

Since we first started spending time together, what is one thing God taught you about Him or about the fruit of His Spirit? With the more than 3,000 choices you make every day, you have many opportunities to say yes to God. Take some time to write down some of the ways you have recently either said yes to God or experienced the fruit of His Spirit in your life.

I said yes to love when _____

_____

I said yes to joy when _____

_____

I said yes to peace when _____

_____

I said yes to patience when _____

_____

I said yes to kindness when _____

_____

I said yes to goodness when _____

_____

I said yes to faithfulness when _____

_____

I said yes to gentleness when _____

_____

I said yes to self-control when _____

_____

I can't see what you wrote—and it's okay if you left some spaces blank. But I hope you're encouraged by what you did write down, by these ways you and God are becoming better friends. I am also very happy and excited for you because I know that if you keep following Jesus, the fruit of His Spirit's work in your heart will mean a life full of God's love and the adventures He has for you!

Finally, I want to remind you of something you already know: Growing fruit takes time.

Now, I have to admit I don't know much about planting a garden or growing fruit. I grew up in the city, and we didn't have a garden. We bought all our fruit and vegetables from the grocery store.

Even still, I do know that fruit doesn't grow overnight. Once a seed has been planted, it takes a while for the sprout to break through the ground, for the stem to grow strong and maybe grow into a big tree or a thick bush or a long vine, and then for that plant to be mature enough to bear fruit.

For example, an apple seed takes up to ten years to grow into a tree that actually produces good apples. And a grapevine needs about three years to develop before any grapes grow on it. That's a long time to wait for a piece of fruit, isn't it?

Clearly, farmers have to be patient. They have to believe that what they plant is going to grow, and they have to be willing to spend time taking care of all they plant. They can't just sit and look at the fields every day. They have work to do.

Similarly, God has planted in your heart His seeds of love, joy, peace, patience, kindness, goodness, faithfulness, gentleness, and self-control. Be patient as you wait for those character traits to become more a part of you and more evident in your life. Walk closely with God, reading His Word and talking to Him throughout the day, and watch the fruit of His Spirit grow in you.

A Yes Girl

by Andrea Evans

I listen to God and follow His plan
Even when I might be the only one to take a stand.
I am confident and brave, and I represent Christ.
Even when it's easier to choose wrong, I choose right.
I do not look to others for approval, validation, or
    self-worth:
I know I was fearfully and wonderfully created from
    the time of my birth.
I serve others with a humble and grateful heart
Knowing that I have been handpicked, chosen, and set
    apart.
I give my all in everything God allows me to do,
Which sometimes means He says it's okay to try some-
    thing new.
I say yes to God's calling on my life;
No matter my age, I want to live in His light.
I will nurture and grow the gifts God gives to me.
I will pray, study, and be open to where He leads.
I am not afraid to go against the world.
In fact, that is exactly what it looks like to be a yes girl.

More Great Harvest House Books by Wynter Pitts

For Girls Like You

This daily devotional helps you discover the truth about yourself—who God says you really are—and helps you experience that truth in your daily life. Each devotion includes a prayer to help you apply the lesson.

You're God's Girl!

Daily devotions written directly to your heart will help you discover God's truth—who He made you to be, how unique and special you are, and how you fit into your world. See yourself through His eyes and allow His truth to make a difference in your life. The *real* you, the *true* you, is amazing!

You're God's Girl! Coloring Book

Take God's amazing truths into your heart as you add color to these cool designs using your crayons, colored pencils, watercolors, or markers. Coloring is a fun way to spend some alone time—or invite some girlfriends over and make it a party.

To learn more about Harvest House books and
to read sample chapters, visit our website:

www.harvesthousepublishers.com

HARVEST HOUSE PUBLISHERS
EUGENE, OREGON